Deity & Death

Deity & Death

Selected Symposium Papers

Edited with an Introduction by
Spencer J. Palmer

VOLUME TWO
IN THE RELIGIOUS STUDIES MONOGRAPH SERIES

Foreword by
Ellis T. Rasmussen

Religious Studies Center
Brigham Young University

Library of Congress Catalog Card Number: 78-60636
ISBN 0-88494-342-9

First Printing, 1978

Lithographed in the United States of America
PUBLISHERS PRESS
Salt Lake City, Utah

To Ernest L. Wilkinson
benefactor and friend

Contents

Foreword

This monograph on deity and death comprises selected papers from a symposium on "Deity, Ways of Worship, and Death" held on the Brigham Young University campus, April 13-14, 1977 — the first such scholarly event sponsored by the newly established Religious Studies Center of Brigham Young University. There were eighteen participants from BYU and other educational institutions in the United States and overseas, including Sri Lanka and Japan.

The papers on ways of worship are not included in this book. Several of these were slide presentations which were difficult to reconstruct and reproduce in printed form.

We express sincere appreciation to all who participated. We wish to make special mention of the fact that Jeffrey R. Holland, Commissioner of Education for the far-flung Church Education System of The Church of Jesus Christ of Latter-day Saints, attended the sessions and presented a very insightful luncheon address. (The full address has been published in *Brigham Young University Studies*.) His assessment of the contributions of the symposium speakers and the potential of the new Religious Studies Center in providing a significant service follows:

> In this day of Church activity which is, by a prophet's declaration, going to take us to every nation, kindred, tongue, and people, we do well to aid that process and facilitate our friendships by sharing here, in just such a symposium, our mutual experience, our knowledge of "countries and of kingdoms" as the Lord has commanded. (D&C 88:79.) Even in the early and difficult days of this

dispensation, with more than enough hardships and temporal travail to go around, the Lord nevertheless urged our forefathers to "study and learn and become acquainted with all good books and with languages, tongues, and people." (D&C 90:15.) In the same way and presumably at the same time, we declare ourselves to be seekers after anything that is "virtuous, lovely, or of good report or praiseworthy." (Thirteenth Article of Faith.) That search is now taking us to countries and kingdoms, cultures and corners of the world our fathers never knew and our grandfathers never dreamed of. The rich opportunities of our time suggest that we move as rapidly and as resolutely into these "new" frontiers as we are able.

I am . . . trying to suggest that what you are doing here today in this comparative religion symposium is not simply a nice intellectual exercise or just another praiseworthy educational experience. For me it is part of a personal dream in terms of what the Center for Religious Studies at BYU may yet do. It is deeply theological, it has eternal implications, and it will play its own part in the process of international brotherhood.*

ELLIS T. RASMUSSEN

*Jeffrey R. Holland, " . . . Of Countries and of Kingdoms," *Brigham Young University Studies*, vol. 18, no. 1 (Fall 1977), 4-5.

Introduction

Death is universally regarded as the supreme crisis of life. Yet it may be the most sacred moment of human experience. This paradox suggests another — an increasing concern for death and dying coupled with a general predisposition to avoid talking about them. It is because of this ambivalence — our concern but our reluctance to talk — that these searching and revealing papers on deity and death take on so much significance.

People differ markedly in how they deal with the shock of death. Death has a significance that may be social, political, economic, religious, or deeply personal. Usually our response to death is a reflection of our view of life, including not only the precious life within each of us as individuals, but also of the marvelous and sometimes mysterious life within the universe as a whole. Thus our conception of death is a reliable indicator of how we relate to deity and the divine. Deity and death are two themes of single concern. And as such, they are common denominators in the otherwise diverse studies of comparative religion which comprise this book.

We begin with an intriguing analysis of Korean, Mormon-American and Jewish customs surrounding death, prepared by Paul Dredge, an anthropologist whose findings include original research carried out in the countryside of South Korea. Dredge provides a number of contrasting variations: for in Korea the approach to death is not primarily theological — in which God is the overruling concern — it is social and humanistic in tone. Korean funeral customs are best understood in terms of social disruption. Ceremonial and symbolic efforts are intended to mend breaches in the structure of society caused by death.

In Korea the interval between death and burial is of symbolic importance. It is assumed that the longer the time elapsed, the more socially prominent are the deceased and his family. Three days is normal. Jewish practice, on the other hand, is to bury the deceased within a twenty-four-hour period, and the interval between death and burial is of no symbolic importance. Muslims, Copts, Koreans, Jews and American Mormons all prefer burial to cremation. Among Koreans, as among so many others, the use of professional mourners is customary. But the overall funerary tone in Korea is different from the dark and somber tones of the Middle East. In Korea the bier is profusely and brightly decorated. The funeral procession from the home to the gravesite includes dancers, singers, and musicians, who have sometimes been drinking and who seem to enjoy their work. Whenever possible the funeral is marked by trappings of prosperity, which are intended to enhance the social standing of the deceased and his surviving relatives.

In times of death, American Mormons are only slightly more involved in ceremony than their non-Mormon neighbors. And they are far less involved than Koreans and Chinese. Yet rituals are an important social cement that serves the function of binding generations and families together and, as Dredge points out, Mormon temple rites fill in any deficiencies of the public funeral rites. Ceremonies in the temples often focus upon the dead; temple ceremonies in which the faithful may participate on a regular basis throughout their adult life allow a person in mourning to be reassured in ways that other Americans are not. Temple ceremonies preserve an awareness of the closeness of the living and the dead. For those trying to cope with loss through death, Mormon temples provide distinct reassurances which give spiritual and social support. They strongly reinforce faith in God, faith in the sanctity and continuity of individual life, and faith in the eternal character of the family.

In his fascinating discussion of beliefs and practices concerning death and dying among the Muslims and Copts of Egypt, Sami Hanna effectively illustrates ways in which these directly relate to attitudes toward deity and the divine. Death in the Middle East is an awesome ordeal. In Islām, one is aware that the hour of death has been fixed by God. The shrouding and burial of the physical remains of the deceased should take place without delay. The "true believer" must be immediately ushered into Allāh's bedazzling presence; the "infidel" must be quickly consigned to his bed of fire, which will be fanned by the hot winds of hell.

The true believer is one whose religion is Islām, whose prophet is Muhammed, and whose sacred book is the Qur'ān. At death, Allāh will send the true believer into the Garden of Paradise where he will be clothed in a celestial garment and given delectable pleasures. But for the "pernicious infidel," the messenger of death will execute Allāh's disapproval and wrath. That man's soul will be scattered and dragged forth "like the dragging of an iron spit through moist wool, tearing the veins. . . ."

In Islām, life is a preparation for death, for facing the justice and glory of God. Death at best is an agonizing event, and funerals are marked by lamentation, resignation, and manifest bereavement. None but Allāh knows the outcome of death. One's fate is in his hands. Hence, even for faithful Shem, the anguish of dying turned his beard from gray to white.

Hanna reports that his first experience with an American funeral in Salt Lake City was very disturbing. He learned that in American-Mormon practice there is a deliberate lapse of several days between death and burial during which time family and friends of the deceased visit the mortuary and participate in a public viewing of the body. Hanna was mystified by the spirit of joyfulness that seemed to prevail at this viewing. In sharp contrast to the foreboding atmosphere of "crying and screaming" he had known at funeral rites in the Middle East, this American meeting was marked by an atmosphere of optimism and friendliness, what Truman Madsen in his paper says is closely analogous to a heart-warming missionary farewell. There was composure and even some smiles. Hanna was startled by the question put by a close relative of the deceased as to whether the body in the casket, which had been cosmetically prepared to look as lifelike as possible, did not indeed look beautiful. The funeral which followed the viewing was simple, personal and brief. After the funeral, the bereaved immediately returned to their normal routines.

In Egypt, by contrast, the funeral is followed by a specified period of mourning during which friends and relatives congregate at the home of the deceased to give and receive condolences, commiserate, and drink refreshments. Food is served for three days, but the period of mourning continues for forty. After forty days, professional mourners are brought in, and on Thursdays thereafter people carry palm branches to the tombs of their ancestors.

In a stimulating paper on Mormon distinctions in death and dying, Truman Madsen suggests that in Mormonism there are several kinds of death but the role of Christ is to overcome them all. He observes that in some world religions the role of deity and questions of immortality are often separated, but in Mormonism they are not. Mormonism equates God, immortality, and resurrection. And in its highest expression, life requires all three.

Some philosophers speak of feeling the constant threat of death, but according to Madsen, Joseph Smith, the American founder of Mormonism, regarded death as the key to personal fulfillment and redemption. Death is not a stark enemy but a passing phase in an eternal journey that began for all in a preexistent spiritual state.

Edward "Ted" Jones urges that whatever else may be said of his scholarly findings on ascension motifs in world religion, men must be willing to admit that supernatural experience is actually possible. Human beings can conceivably ascend to heaven and enjoy a foretaste of deity and the divine while still on earth. In a thoroughgoing analysis of ascension stories in five major religious traditions — Hebrew, Christian, Muslim, Hindu, and Buddhist — Jones cites numerous reports of pious and faithful people having been taken into the presence of God before tasting death, having received divine revelation, and having been miraculously translated so as not to have to endure the ordeal of death at all.

Jones has discovered a number of common patterns in these various ascension experiences: death is not the end of life, but a new beginning; there are many heavens and hells, and as one progresses upward, one faces greater light; when the faithful are ushered into the presence of God, they receive previously hidden knowledge in the form of new symbols, keys, and crowns; divine authority and power is granted; one obtains perfect union with

God; and the holy experience of entering into God's presence can have vicarious benefits for others, the dead as well as the living.

In Mormon theology all life is precious, and the innumerable living beings of the universe are sacred. They deserve respect and reverence, and it is on the basis of these beliefs that Gerald Jones suggests a legitimate comparison between "ahimsa" and certain elements in Mormon thought.

All the religions of India stress the importance of reverence for life, but Jainism has always been the most fervent supporter of this doctrine of non-injury (ahimsa) toward living beings. Buddhism does not allow for life in plants in the sense that gods, human beings or animals have life. Jainism and Mormonism, however, find spirits not only in plants but in the earth and the very elements of earth. In Mormon scripture, as Madsen observes, the earth itself is a living entity, a body actuated by a spirit. That body has been baptized, must be sanctified by fire, and will eventually die and pass into a new phase.

In some Asian faiths the spirit suffers under the weight of material bondage, and acts of selfishness and injury, violence, murder, killing and cruelty are by far the most damaging. Proscriptions against those are most common. Jain monks vow that they will not deliberately harm even microscopic life in earth, water, fire, or wind. They strain their drinking water in order to avoid harming the spirit entities within it, and they carry fly whisks to clear the path before them in order to avoid stepping on unnoticed insects or bugs. Jones explains that their ahimsa, their reverence for all life, leads to a wide-ranging asceticism, including a strict vegetarian diet.

Mormon reverence for life does not go to such extremes, but it is important. After tracing ahimsa motifs in Hebrew, Greek, and Puritan thought, Jones shows that Mormon scriptures and the teachings of Church leaders not only strongly oppose murder and violence and have frequently denounced war, but have urged kindness and respect for animal life (even venomous snakes), restraints in eating meat, and abstinence from food and drink on the first Sunday of each month. And this fasting is to be accompanied by compassion and prayer, and by giving financial assistance to those in need.

Hinduism, Buddhism, and Jainism regard the body as an impediment to spiritual life. Salvation is to be found in freeing the spirit (soul) from matter, that it may regain its pristine purity and enjoy bliss. Mormons believe that the whole world is alive with individual spirit beings which inhabit physical bodies. However, where Jains and others may believe that the spirits are chained to matter and must gain release, Mormons teach that God has made provision for physical bodies to be placed on earth precisely for the purpose of receiving spirits. To be alive in this physical world is a great blessing, absolutely prerequisite to individual immortality, whether for animals, plants, or man. In Mormon belief the purpose of life is to transform the flesh, not to mortify it, that man may become more like God, who himself has a celestialized body of flesh and bones.

Seiji Katanuma's delightful essay is concerned with the role of the many gods in ancient Japanese religion. He views them through reference to the earliest religious texts, the Kojiki and the Nihongi. It is a picture far different from that of China, for the Japan of legend is an eight-island country of splendor and brightness, of towering mountains and shimmering streams, of brilliant sun, languid moon and glittering stars, and fields of rice with golden shafts. Japan is the land of the kami, the nature gods. Its religion is Shinto, the way of the gods. In traditional Shinto there is no supreme absolute, no transcendent creator god, no creed, no founder of faith, no metaphysical goal, no sin, no devil, no concern with resurrection, no explanation of life after death. There is only a consciousness of light as opposed to darkness, purity as opposed to filthiness, and a wide variety of customs and folkways on how to gain a beautiful mind and to appreciate and honor the awesome powers of nature. In short, it is showing respect for kami.

Among the ancient Japanese, the world of death was called the country of the tree-roots — a place which lay far beyond the fields of flowing rice shafts. But there was no doctrine to explain who would go to the dark place — the country of roots — and who would not.

Philosophical questions dealing with death, or the ultimate state of nirvana, were introduced into Japan from India via China and Korea at the beginning of the sixth century. In the end, these new Buddhist ideas addressed questions of being and life after death, which Shinto continued to slight or ignore. But in time native Shinto, with its focus on the kami, developed a "monarchical mystique" based on the worship of an imperial family which traced its lineage back to Amaterasu, the kami of the sun. The process by which this was accomplished is of primary concern in Katanuma's research.

In his insightful essay on "Chinese Modes of Objectifying Divine Power," the concluding paper in this collection, Laurence Thompson cautions that there is always the hazard of constructing easy and spurious analogies between religious systems and suggests that it is particularly self-defeating to attempt to understand Chinese views of deity and the divine from the vantage point of traditional Western theological concepts. This caution has also been voiced by some Jewish scholars who maintain that Judaism, unlike Christianity, is not really a religion, or that creedal religion is only a small part of the totality of what is involved in being a Jew. From this standpoint, Christians frequently run the risk of imposing an exterior system of categories on an inherently organic Judaic "system" because that religion is a mixture of folk and faith, culture and tradition, and law and history that is difficult to define and cannot be explained by the citation of a creed. This argument is sometimes applied to Mormonism, which is characterized as a way of life, a religion without catechism or creed, and one committed to progressive revelation.

Thompson differentiates between Chinese, Western, and Indian views of divine power. For the biblical faiths of the West (Christianity, Judaism, and Islam), God is outside and above nature; he is the creator and man is his creation. In India, God and creation are the same. But among the Chinese, the problem of the divine is more ambiguous, or at least more complex. At the philosophical level among the Chinese, man and nature are part of a great whole, a gestalt; ultimate reality is not a personal deity, it is Tao. And Tao is neither worshipped nor objectified. Yet at the popular level, there is ample room for personified gods. As in Mormonism and Japanese Shinto, Chinese deities apparently proliferate and counsel together. In Chinese popular religion, polytheism is pronounced. This polytheism stands in marked contrast to most other major Western religions which are characterized by a belief in only one true God.

In Chinese religion there are numerous demons (kuei), but there is no transcendental struggle between good and evil, no strict duality between evil forces and God so characteristic of the Christian world, and it might be added, of Mormonism. Rather, Tao is one. Tao is abstract and mystical, and overarches all. There is no exact equivalent of Tao in Mormon thought, although "the light of truth" and "the light of Christ" (D&C 88:6 ff) sometimes seem to approach it. Thompson posits that in Chinese religion there is no principle or power of evil at large in the universe of which malevolent spirits are agents. Rather, the countless malign spirits, so widely acknowledged at the folk level, are ghosts of humans who have proven to be a menace to the community because of their bitter resentment at having been abandoned by descendants who failed to perform vicarious ancestral rites.

SPENCER J. PALMER

Death and Dying

What's in a Funeral? Korean, American-Mormon and Jewish Rites Compared

1

C. Paul Dredge

Words are symbols we use to communicate with, but they are not the only communicative symbols in the human repertoire. Ritual practices — both religious and secular — embody myriad symbols which, like words, have meanings that are grounded in contrast and likeness as well as in actual experience (both conscious and unconscious) and which therefore communicate certain messages to both participants and observers associated with ritual activity. Of the symbolic systems that impart meaning to ritual, the anthropologist Edmund Leach says that

> . . . symbols occur in sets and . . . the meaning of particular symbols is to be found in the contrast with other symbols rather than in the symbol as such.

And also:

> The indices in non-verbal communication systems, like the sound elements in spoken language, do not have meaning as isolates, but only as members of sets. (Leach 1976:59, 112)

Like words, the meaning of ritual symbols is dependent upon contrast and likeness to other symbols in the same system and in associated systems. An example to be found in the Mormon ritual complex is the association of baptism, partaking of the sacrament, burial, birth, and resurrection — all of which are juxtaposed in contrast and likeness to give each of them a symbolic meaning that they could not otherwise have.

Of particular social significance are the rituals anthropologists usually call "the rites of passage." (Van Gennep 1960) Rites of passage, which mark a transition from one stage of human life to the next, are common in all societies. They include such rites as christenings, circumcision, puberty rites, marriages, and funerals.[1] My analysis here will be limited to a brief and clearly incomplete discussion of aspects of funeral rites, their symbolic meanings, and the functions they provide, both social and psychological. In attempting to make a cross-cultural comparison and because of space limitations, the "forest of symbols" (after Turner 1967) will receive less than full treatment — a few important old trees will be the limit. The comparison presented here deals with American-Mormon, rural Korean, and some aspects of Jewish funerals. While the ideal discussion of such rites should include visual illustration of the funeral rites of each of these three cultures, verbal description will have to suffice. My own firsthand observations serve as the primary sources for describing Mormon and Korean funerals, while the description of Jewish funeral practices is based on research into textual sources and on term papers written by several Jewish students for a course on death and dying.

Although it is a somewhat arbitrary division, the symbols of a funeral can be divided into three parts. First, religious symbols point to beliefs about life after death and the influence of the dead on the living. Second, social symbols portray relationships between the dead and the living and among the living. Observing and interpreting social symbols can be called the "Moscow-on-May-Day" approach, since like analysts of the Soviet scene, we look at who stands where, who is present, and who is absent. If the analysts of the Soviet order can get an idea of the social order in the Kremlin from watching parades and processions, we can likewise acquire insights into the social order of the community by observing the ritual order. Third, since death is a universal feature of the human experience, the comparison of funeral symbolism cross-culturally transforms those symbols into what I call macro-social symbols. The analysis of these macro-social symbols helps to draw general conclusions about the nature of different cultures and brings into better focus the meaning of particular religious and social symbols. It is also useful to at least attempt to draw from these symbols some generalizations concerning humanity in general with regard to death and mourning.

The functions of ritual communication center on social and psychological influences. Social functions can either be conscious and even manipulated, such as the sending of flowers of a certain kind and expense in order to create a desired impression, or unconscious, such as the unstated feelings of solidarity and community which are created or reinforced by group participation in ritual activity. The psychological functions of concern here are those which have to do with individual adjustment to the reality of death — grief and mourning and the reintegration of the bereaved into normal life.

As mentioned above, the meanings of some of the symbols and their functions may not be grasped at the conscious level for the participants in a funeral.[2] The unconscious nature of the meaning of such symbols does not keep them from being extremely compelling and influential. The anthropologist who does a symbolic analysis of a ritual takes this fact into account in his methodology, which consists ideally of three basic components. The first is the observation and recording of actual ritual performance. It is useful to take photographs, especially moving pictures, so that details of the ritual which are overlooked in the first observation can be identified in subsequent review. Also, since each ritual is an event unique unto itself, a series of the same kind of rituals will provide a more clear picture of what the ideal performance should be, just as attending more than one game at Fenway Park is necessary before the rules of baseball and the pecking order of the Boston Red Sox become clear.

The second basic component of methodology in ritual analysis is to elicit the interpretations of the participants, both as written in texts and as expressed orally. While some analysts tend to discount native interpretations (cf. Levi-Strauss 1963), it is usually true that participants' views can be very enlightening if only for the reason that what they perceive as true influences their behavior and the meaning they ascribe to ritual actions.

Third, the methodology of the anthropologist should include a full contextual analysis, an attempt to put an individual ritual performance in a perspective built on thorough understanding of the entire ethnographic complex. Hence, the anthropologist must be responsible for a knowledge of other religious rites, belief systems, social structure, political and economic forces, language and speech customs, and available historical records which pertain to the culture he is analyzing. Without a broad knowledge of ethnographic detail, the anthropologist's insights will not take him further than what his informants have told him, and without transcending that native exegetic model of the ritual, he will not be able to get at the meanings which unconsciously motivate the feelings and actions of participants.

Funerals, as well as some other rites of passage, "create a social event out of a natural fact" (Malinowski 1954:52) and "convert the obligatory (and inevitable) into the desirable" (Turner 1967:30) through the use of symbolic communication. The onset of puberty or the occurrence of death are natural and inevitable (marriage is obligatory). But in order to cope with them, to live with the new situation and accept its reality and the new responsibilities, statuses, relationships, and emotions (often fear and misgiving) they entail, rites of passage transform the reality of these transitions into both social events, in which many can share the burden and reinforce the new order, and desirable facts, such as in the emphasis on joy and happiness at weddings and the deemphasis on the inevitable and sometimes frightening separations and challenges a wedding presents to the bride and groom. The pageantry of a funeral often supports the notion that being dead is better than the alternative, although it would be difficult to hold that opinion if the death had not already taken place.

Van Gennep outlines three stages in a rite of passage: (1) separation, (2) transition, and (3) incorporation. In a funeral, these stages are more difficult to identify than in puberty and initiation rites but can generally be associated with funeral procedures in the following way: separation is the actual death itself and the preparation of the body for disposal; the entire funeral ceremony can be said to constitute the transition stage; and incorporation is the procession to the place of disposal (the territory of the dead) and the actual burial, cremation, or abandonment of the body. In all stages, the deceased *and* the mourners are directly involved, as well as other members of the community; and, more than in some others rites of passage, the secondary actors rather than the deceased are the foci of many of the rites. When the process is completed, the mourners and deceased all stand in a slightly or perhaps substantially *new* and *different* relationship to each other. The deceased has a new status, that of decedent, which can often be as influential in the social world as his previous status was during his lifetime, since his widow, heir, and other survivors will be expected to substantially alter their behavior. (Vernon 1970)

Death and Funeral Preparations

In Korea, death occurs at home. When people are hospitalized for a serious chronic illness, every effort is made to bring them home to die so that their spirits will not wander and become disoriented — unhappy ancestral spirits make for bad family fortune. When death occurs, the women of the family immediately commence a loud wailing, "*aigu, aigu*" for a parent and "*oi, oi*" for another relation. This wailing seldom ceases during the period before burial. Someone is always with the corpse, a duty that is important because the spirit of the dead is still nearby and not yet at rest — the body still has importance to the spirit(s) that has left it and therefore to the survivors. The relatives are notified by foot messenger and through the mail, while those in the community learn from the sounds emanating from the home that a death has occurred. Relatives who live nearby rush to the scene to begin making arrangements and cooking the food that will be necessary to feed the funeral guests.

In the United States, chances are that the person will die in the hospital (approximately 70 percent die in some sort of institution), often unattended by anyone he knows well. Relatives will be notified by phone and the funeral director will take care of newspaper obituaries so that the community will be informed. Arrangements for the funeral and burial will be made by the specialist. Like the experience of witnessing birth in the United States, the observation of dying and death is seldom direct; the stark realities of these vital processes are mediated by institutions and privacy to the extent that many Americans are able to avoid almost any firsthand experience with them. We are a nation of middlemen and specialists with chains of responsibility, distribution, production, and information that allow us only fragmentary experience with many life processes; so to be half a step removed from birth or death is a natural feature of our unnatural culture. Even when a family member is present in the hospital, the death of a loved one demands silence and control, not wailing and emotional release.

Jewish people find a middle ground, with an individual who is suited and willing as the bedside attendant, faithful in his vigil until the moment of death. Like the Korean fear of dying in a strange place, the Jewish aversion to dying alone requires a member of the family at the deathbed, even if that bed is in a terminal cancer ward of a hospital. Of course, fears of loneliness and separation from home are most likely basic to humans everywhere, but the lack of a cultural prescription to deal with them often surrenders the dying to the impersonal ministry of medical technology. Those who may feel a responsibility nonetheless often abdicate in the hope that a professional, because he is supposedly better able to deal with what he must face daily, will fill their duties of final ministration. This tendency has become so prevalent that nurses and even doctors are currently being trained, as part of their regular career preparation, to deal with the social and psychological aspects of dying and the total (as opposed to merely physical) care of terminal patients. In short, the skills they are assumed to have are now being developed because that assumption has made them necessary. (See Kübler-Ross 1969, Hinton 1976)

Time is often symbolic. In funeral practices, the time between death and burial often expresses a message beyond mere practicality and necessity. Traditionally, Korean funerals were held three, five, seven, or nine days after the death of a person, depending on his social status. The longer the interval, the more prominent the citizen. This rule also had the function of providing for funeral guests to arrive from long distances, a more likely consideration for a decedent of wide power and associations. With the decline of class distinctions, most Korean funerals today are held on the third day after death (like the Biblical third day, the calculation includes the day of death, even if the person dies at 11:59 P.M.). True to tradition, however, the funeral of Mrs. Park Chung Hee, who was assassinated in August of 1974, the wife of Korea's President Park, was held on the fifth day. By contrast, such time considerations seem to have little symbolic value in American society. Three days is normal unless something like the return of a son or daughter from a distant place causes the funeral to be postponed. Time is an important element in Jewish funerals, since the Jewish practice is to bury the person within twenty-four hours of death. Delay is an insult to the deceased, because the onset of decomposition in the traditionally unembalmed body is regarded as a terrible humiliation and insult to the deceased if it is allowed to begin before the placing of the body in the ground.

Upon death, survivors in any culture are left with the problem of what to do with the body of the deceased. Prescriptive cultural understandings provide a usual procedure for this task, which may be complex or quite simple but usually must begin in its early stages immediately after death. Malinowski has voiced important insights concerning this task:

> The emotions [regarding the dead and his body] are extremely complex and even contradictory; the dominant elements, love of the dead and loathing of the corpse, passionate attachment to the personality still lingering about the body and a shattering fear of the gruesome thing that has been left over, these two elements seem to mingle and play into each other.
>
> . . . the two-fold contradictory tendency, on the one hand to preserve the body, to keep its form intact, or to retain parts of it; on the other hand the desire to be done with it, to put it out of the way, to annihilate it completely. Mummification and burning are the two extreme expressions of this two-fold

> tendency. . . . in these customs is clearly expressed the fundamental attitude of mind of the surviving relative, friend or lover, the longing for all that remains of the dead person and the disgust and fear of the dreadful transformation wrought by death. (Malinowski 1948:48-50)

In earlier times in America, the custom was to keep a lock of hair of the deceased in a glass bell jar in the home, a clear manifestation of the reluctance to part with the body of the deceased. Malinowski states that one of the more interesting results of the conflict of attitudes he explains above is the gruesome custom of sarco-cannibalism in Melanesia. The flesh of the dead person is eaten, in piety, by his relatives, a practice which is regarded as a "supreme act of reverence, love and devotion." (1948:50) At the same time, it is done with extreme repugnance and aversion, often accompanied by violent vomiting. A rather mild act by comparison, the kissing of a dead mother's cheek by her daughters at a Mormon funeral I once attended illustrated the same conflicting attitudes. After one daughter had bestowed the kiss, she urged the others to do so as well. They conformed to her wishes in response to this challenge to their devotion, while clearly feeling repugnance at the thought of kissing a dead person.

All three traditions under discussion here prefer burial to cremation, but the preparation of the body before final disposition differs somewhat in each case. Koreans wash the body in incense water and dress it in a set of clothes especially prepared for use in burial. The ears and nose are plugged with cotton, coins are placed over the eyes, three spoonfuls of rice are placed in the mouth, the thumbs and toes are tied together so that the body will fit the narrow coffin, the body is arranged to face south — the proper direction for homes and cities to face also, into the sun — a quilt is placed over the body, and a folding screen is put up to shield the body from view. Family members are free to view the corpse if they wish, but it is extremely unusual for those who pay condolences at the home before the funeral procession to view the remains.

American Mormons follow the custom of their communities in having bodies embalmed, although, contrary to popular opinion, embalming is not a legal requirement in all states. (Massachusetts, for instance, has a law that requires embalming only in cases where the body must be transported over great distances by public conveyance.) The preservation of a body through embalming may reflect the Mormon religious belief in a literal physical resurrection, although there is no doctrine which indicates that steps should be taken to preserve the remains intact or in one place, and the practice of embalming is not peculiarly Mormon. Mormons also participate in viewing the corpse as part of the funeral process. Funeral directors will usually say that confrontation with the reality of death through the viewing of the corpse is good emotional therapy for the bereaved because it helps them to accept the finality of death and move on to a realistic and constructive adjustment to life without the deceased. At the same time, embalming fluid contains red dye to restore color, and this basic cosmetic preparation is combined with extensive efforts at makeup and other attempts at beautification that tend to disguise the true nature of death and, some would say, aid in its denial. The function of embalming is therefore ambiguous and its symbolism is open to debate. It does fit into the system of specialization which characterizes industrial societies. In comparison, the steps for preparing a body for burial in Korea are outlined in ritual handbooks available to anyone, handbooks which also contain instructions for the proper procedures at weddings, funerals, and ancestor veneration ceremonies in an instructional mode similar to that of handbooks on etiquette in America. Mormon Relief Society leadership manuals still contain instructions on the subject of preparation of the dead for burial, but the decline in the need for this service has meant that the instructions are less detailed in recent editions than they formerly were.

In the Jewish tradition, the body is prepared for burial in a procedure called the *taharah*. All parts of the body are washed with warm water while prayers and psalms are recited. Formerly the function of a family member, the *taharah* is now performed most often by a funeral director who must be acquainted with the details of the ceremony (and probably be Jewish himself) or by an organization known as the *Hevra kaddisha* (Holy society), a burial society formed of prominent and pious Jewish community members to insure proper burial and remove profit and commercialism in dealing with the dead. During the *taharah,* great care is taken to prevent the face of the deceased from looking downward, a serious sign of disrespect for the dead. The act of performing the *taharah* is regarded as a *mitzvah,* a deed of true charity, since the recipient of the service cannot repay the giver. Jewish tradition discourages embalming, since the decomposition of the body and its return to the earth are seen as natural and necessary processes. In a case where embalming is done, blood and other body fluids are retained and buried with the body. (See Lamm 1969)

Clothing

Clothing associated with funerals is often highly symbolic, both in the case of burial clothing and mourning attire. In Korea, it is customary to prepare burial clothing well in advance of need, an act of filial piety on the part of adult children which shows respect and love for aging parents and assures them that a funeral will be properly conducted. The clothing itself is made of fine-quality material and is usually a subdued grey in color, like the clothing worn by the elderly while they are alive. The color is significant as it fits into the spectrum of traditional clothing styles and colors throughout the life cycle. A bride wears a red skirt and a green jacket, symbolic of life and fertility. Her clothing becomes more subdued in color as she gets older, finally centering on the subdued grey of the elderly which is also worn by Buddhist monks and nuns in Korea (who are usually celibate and who often inhabit a liminal world between the living and the dead). So from an apex of fertility and life at marriage, a person slowly moves toward a loss of fertility and the withdrawal from more and more activities of life in a gradual decline toward a natural end.

In contrast to most Americans, Mormons often receive burial clothing as gifts long before it is needed for that purpose. That such clothing is also used in temple ceremonies, and is therefore useful outside the context of death, does not totally negate the death-related significance of it. Few Americans can expect to be sent to the grave in clothing which, in some cases at least, their mothers made many years before, but this is not unusual for

Mormon people. The feelings upon receipt of such a gift are not substantially different from those of the Korean parent who receives the gift of burial clothing, although the uses to which the temple clothing is put are more diverse. The Mormon clothing is highly symbolic, associated with temple ritual and various religious doctrines. In contrast to the Korean burial clothing, Mormons go to the grave wearing what could be regarded as a symbol of fertility — an appropriate symbolic expression of their belief in eternal increase. It is also of interest to note that burial clothing is the same as wedding clothing for Mormons, a feature of burials in parts of the American South in the past (Faulkner 1930) and a practice that corresponds with some features of Korean burial customs.

Jewish burial clothing consists of a three-piece shroud made of white linen. Like the Mormon clothing, it is the same for all people, symbolizing the equality of all before God. It is a stated requirement that the shroud have no pockets, a sign that no material goods can be taken to the other side. A white prayer shawl is sometimes included in the burial attire, but with one or more of the fringes removed to symbolize the new status of the wearer. The prayer shawl is often worn by the deceased before his death.

Korean mourning attire is by far the most complex of the three cultures. As illustrated in tables which are included in the funeral section of ritual handbooks, mourning dress varies according to the kinship relations between the mourner and the deceased. With the stated intent of discouraging excessive spending on funerals, a recent law has changed the type of clothing worn by those who are mourning, but the basic system has remained intact. Mourning clothes are currently made of slightly bleached hemp, a rather finely woven sort of sackcloth, and consist for men of four main parts: a cap, a coat, leggings, and straw shoes. Sons and grandsons all wear the full apparel, while unmarried daughters and granddaughters, daughters-in-law, and wives all wear the corresponding apparel for women. Nephews and cousins of the deceased wear the cap and the leggings at the funeral, but not the coat or the straw shoes, and relatives of the fifth and sixth degree, according to Korean reckoning (first cousins once removed and second cousins), wear only the cap. This group of kinsmen and the seventh and eighth degree relatives, who must attend a funeral but are not required to wear mourning clothes, make up a kinship group called the *tangnae*. The *tangnae* is the Korean unit of close kinship, involved in not only mourning responsibilities, but also in other sorts of mutual aid and ritual participation. It is interesting to note that speech between members of this kindred (for each *tangnae* group will be different for each individual) differs significantly from that between more distant kinsmen — a further correlation of the symbol of their closeness embodied in mourning attire. The traditional ideal was to wear mourning clothes for three years after the death of a parent and to live apart from normal society during that time, although few were financially able to make such sacrifices of potential labor. Today, it is unusual for mourners to continue to wear mourning attire after the funeral, except in the case of widows, who usually dress in white for a mourning period of one year. Sons and daughters of the deceased often pin small patches of the hempen cloth to their regular clothing as token indications of mourning while continuing to participate in normal activities. The participation of principal mourners in ancestral rites is forbidden, however, because of the belief that the deceased was lost by reason of their negligence, making such persons, therefore, ritually polluted.

Guilt, Penance, and Discomfort

The traditionally undyed or currently rough white color of Korean mourning clothes symbolizes the poverty of one who has lost a close relative as well as the liminality of the mourner's position in the life cycle, as described above in reference to color symbolism in burial clothing. Since a person in mourning was traditionally supposed to isolate himself from normal living until his period of mourning was over, his clothing represented and continues to symbolize this withdrawal from everyday activity. Traditional mourning customs also stipulate that during the mourning period the bereaved are to restrict their diets rather severely and thus should carry canes to support them in their weakness. Hence the cane, a part of the mourning apparel which the recent law has declared obsolete and unnecessary, is a sign of coming weakness caused by fasting and decreased food intake.

The black clothing that is traditional for mourners in the West can be seen as symbolic of several concepts. If a bride wears white as a sign of purity, a widow wears black as a sign of her uncleanliness and of her own nearness to death. The historical background of black as a color of mourning is said to be associated with the fear of the ghost of the dead returning. By wearing black, the survivors could render themselves invisible to the ghosts of the dead, who were believed to come out only at night. The home of the deceased was also decorated in black in past years, with a black wreath on the door and the shades pulled. Mirrors were turned to the wall — a concern with beauty was regarded as an insult to the dead, since he was not beautiful and could not do anything to remedy that situation. Most of these practices have been abandoned today, although mirrors are still turned to the wall in Jewish households. Even the symbolic representation of death is something to avoid in our time. We seem, as Americans, to have become afraid or at least reluctant to face death. The applicability of such an assessment for Mormons, however, is subject to considerable doubt. If Mormons are willing to give up the trappings of mourning and bereavement, perhaps they are doing nothing more than following the admonition in the Bible to "let the dead bury their dead," firm in the knowledge that those who die have only gone on to a new stage of life.

Jewish practice for the close relatives of the deceased is to tear their clothing at the moment of the death or news of the death, an act called the *keriah*. This custom provides a symbol of mourning, for the tear should not be more than superficially mended during the year of restricted activity which close family members should observe. For a son or a daughter, the tear should be over the heart, and for siblings, parents, or a spouse, it should be over the right breast. Tearing of clothing is also seen as an outlet for the emotions in a time of intense grief, and orthodox writers normally criticize the more recent custom of pinning a torn piece of cloth over the appropriate spot as a degenerate and unworthy practice.

Further Preparations – the Coffin

In a Korean village, relatives of the deceased place him in the plain pine coffin and prepare for the funeral procession. A woman's marriage document is placed in the coffin with her so that, as one informant told me, she will be married in the afterlife as well. This practice is comparable to that of burial in wedding attire, as mentioned above. Other possessions, such as eyeglasses, a pipe, and a small purse of coins, are put in before the lid is nailed shut. A picture of the deceased and a paper tablet with his/her name on it are prepared for the procession and for the numerous rites which follow the funeral proper. These objects will house the soul of the deceased on the way to the grave so that he will not linger in the village.

Coffins in Korea are intended to rot away quickly so that the bones of the deceased can be exhumed, cleaned, and set in their final resting place directly in the earth. This contrasts with the very common use of metal caskets and airtight vaults in American burials, including those used by Mormons. Coffins for orthodox Jews must be made entirely of wood, even to the point that wooden pegs rather than nails should be used in their construction. Jewish cemeteries permit burial without a vault so that the coffin will rot quickly and the remains will decompose and return to the earth.

Among American Mormons, the final closing of the casket is a time of family togetherness, when the patriarch of the family, often the patrilineal successor to the deceased, pronounces the family prayer — a farewell and blessing for the deceased and his survivors. The final good-bye to the remains is often an extremely emotional time, and its restriction to members of the close family allows for a less inhibited show of feelings. One's duty is to be present for this event, if a member of the immediate family, and to be absent is a sign of irresponsibility. Kinship is, after all, a pact built of both love and fear — fear of being alone or having no one to help in a crisis. Failure to be present at critical stages of a funeral is to renounce that pact, to refuse to reciprocate the faithfulness of the deceased, and to relinquish claim to the faithful attendance of other members of the family when they are most needed. I believe that it was for these reasons, although unstated at the time, that my mother was extremely upset with me when I missed the family prayer for my grandfather (I was only seven years old at the time). My own reaction was to feel very guilty and to learn that at the next opportunity I would feel better by behaving in the proper way. The symbolism and the function contained in any aspect of funeral ritual may not be openly stated or even consciously realized, but the reaction is swift when people behave improperly so as to detract from the symbol or inhibit its function.

The Funeral and the Procession

Much can be learned from close scrutiny of the Korean funeral procession. There is no eulogy or funeral service per se; condolences have been paid individually to the family members and to the spirit of the deceased (bowing to the picture of the deceased two times is the proper expression of respect, then one bow to the chief mourners and a word of condolence), and the guests have been served a meal which includes many delicacies and wine. In the late morning the coffin is brought out of the house and secured to the bier with seven lashes of straw rope which has been made by twisting straw in reverse of the normal direction, a symbol of the inverted status of the dead. In a rural village, the bottom framework of the bier, which will provide the means of the bearers' carrying the coffin, is always community property. The decorative part of the bier may or may not be a communally owned object. In many areas of Korea, the bier is constructed of thin wood and paper, brightly colored and decorated with pictures of beings from the world of spirits where the deceased will begin his new life. Where the decorative portion of the bier is purchased for each individual funeral, it is possible to make a show of wealth and to purchase the best of three models commonly available (single, double, and triple tiered decorations). Hence the design of the bier becomes a symbol of wealth and of prestige, and along with the food provided for the guests becomes an indicator of the social status of the deceased and his family.

A canopy is placed over the bier, reminiscent of the canopies used for weddings and for ancestor veneration rites in the spring and autumn. The canopy denotes the sacred nature of the activities performed beneath it and is seen also as the covering for a temporary shrine for the deceased where those paying their respects bow to the picture and tablet of the deceased. On the two corners of the canopy that cover the front of the bier (where the head of the deceased is located), two characters are attached, written on white paper. The first means "respect" and the second is a charm character with no particular meaning, except that the handbooks say that it should be attached to the front of the bier. In front of the bier proper is carried the spirit chair or house, in which are kept the picture of the deceased and the tablet (paper or wooden) upon which is written his name. Preceding both of these are two banners, one red with the inscription written in silver: "The late scholar Kim of Kimhae (or other lineage designation) — his coffin," and the other a piece of hempen cloth similar in size to that of the red banner which will be used to wipe the dirt off the top of the coffin and cover it before the actual burial.

The people who carry the banners, the spirit house, and the bier itself were traditionally servant-class people. When Korea was liberated from Japanese control at the end of World War II, the old class structure was gradually broken down, partially by means of a land reform law which gave land which formerly belonged to gentry-class landlords to the servants and tenants of those landlords. With financial freedom, the former servants did not have to demean themselves with the ritually polluting chores of coffin bearing, which left the gentry to do it for themselves.

Burial societies were formed by sons on behalf of their parents, and now when someone dies, his bier is borne by the members, or their sons, of the burial association. Still, the bearers wear small white hats which are paper imitations of the kerchief caps worn by the servants of old, and they take the same opportunities as the servants used to take to extort extra rewards for their efforts at a time when the bereaved can least afford to deny them. Each bridge and every intersection along the route to the grave is an opportunity to balk and demand cigarettes or money or wine, and the mourners come prepared to meet such demands as they follow the bier along the path. The banner carriers in the funerals I witnessed were men who still held servant status and were subject, by their own agreement, to the indignities of such a social situation — in exchange, of course, for a secure livelihood. Hence the funeral procession in a Korean village today is a depiction of both the old social order and some of the changes that have taken place in recent years.

If the class structure symbolized in a Korean funeral procession is now virtually gone, the relationships between kinsmen as they are illustrated in mourning dress and position in the procession are quite faithfully presented in symbol. By the time the procession begins, the wailing of the women is also more symbolic than real, since by the third day of wailing, most are too exhausted to feel very intense emotion. Women are usually allowed to follow the bier only as far as the edge of the village boundary; the function of this practice is explained as the protection of the women from the strain of a long trek up the mountainside to the burial site. Their exclusion from this activity does, however, correlate with other symbols of their marginal membership in the lineages into which they are either born or have married. A woman is always either about to leave the lineage through marriage, and is hence an inferior member of it, or has come from outside the lineage in the process of marriage, and is therefore a person of divided loyalties. Traditionally, a woman only goes all the way to the grave in her own casket, and students of Korean lineages and kinship structure state that it is indeed only at her death that she becomes a true member of her husband's lineage. (Lee 1975)

Those with no ties of kinship who follow the bier to the grave are expressing their friendship and allegiance to either the deceased or members of his family. When most of the population of one village is made up of members of a single lineage, it is also a sign of village solidarity to attend the funeral and join the procession.[3]

The funeral procession, in Cholla province at least, normally stops by the roadside just outside the village for a final pause before the actual trip to the gravesite. This is the final chance for latecomers to pay their condolences and to be feasted. All those who attend a funeral are expected to make a donation to the family in memory of the deceased. These offerings, which can sometimes be rather large where the donor is trying to curry favor with the survivors, are used to defray the costs of the funeral. It is a rare funeral which does not pay for itself in this manner. The gesture of friendship functions as a form of life insurance with each family collecting in time of need and donating small amounts as others are in need of assistance.

Occasionally, the bier of the deceased will be decorated in white only with none of the colorful gaiety of the usual ''flower bier.'' Those in white are being buried in a state of ritual mourning for a relative, often a husband, and go to the grave in their mourning attire. Such is the strength of mourning obligations.

Behind the spirit house, and preceding the bier, walk the leaders of the chant recounting the good deeds of the deceased and expressing hope for his well-being on the other side. Bells are rung to attract the attention of the spirit and keep him on the road out of the village. The chant is practiced the night before the funeral by the bearers. The sound of the dirge echoes across the valley deep into the night, sometimes audible for several miles in the country silence, reminding all who hear of the funeral on the morrow and the inevitability of their own end. Well rehearsed, the chant leaders and the bearers are better able to address the spirit of the dead the next day, when their efforts must be successful.

The funeral procession at any American funeral, including a Mormon one, is also highly informative from a symbolic point of view. The order of the cars in a procession, at least where the family is concerned, symbolizes the relationships between the deceased and his relatives — those closest to the hearse are also the closest in terms of kinship. While this is obvious to any person who has attended a funeral, it is not trivial. Places in a funeral procession, like positions in a wedding line, are important indicators of relationships, and if a person finds himself in a position where he feels his status is symbolized as less than it should be, he will often express dissatisfaction, or at least *feel* as though his position has been denigrated. From another point of view, the order of the funeral procession is a rough approximation of the order of heirs to the estate of one who dies intestate, provided that all are in attendance who should be. The correspondence is not accidental. Unlike the Korean procession, which moves at a very slow and halting pace (whether due to the fatigue of the bearers and their harassment of the mourners or because the journey to the grave is a reluctant one — the reason is not clear), the motorcade drives purposefully, perhaps slowly but with no stops, to the cemetery. Most states have laws to allow funeral processions to ignore red lights and stop signs, and many communities provide a police escort to insure the safety of this practice. In Massachusetts, a funeral procession is required to stop for only one reason: to allow a wedding procession to pass. A Korean funeral procession which must pass along a major road in the countryside may tie up traffic for hours, since it need not relinquish the right of way for even a bus-full of people going to market. Such situations are particularly good for extorting more gifts from the mourners, if the bearers deem them able to afford it, and also from those whose passage in a bus or other vehicle is being blocked.

Like the number of layers on the bier and the quality and quantity of food served in the Korean case, American funerals can be said to be more or less opulent according to the amount of money spent on certain necessary items. The casket and flower offerings are the best cases in point. A funeral director is quoted in the following comment:

> A funeral is not an occasion for cheapness. It is, in fact, an opportunity for the display of a status symbol which, by bolstering family pride, does much to assuage grief. . . . It seems highly probable that the most satisfying funeral service for the average family is one in which the costs has necessitated some degree of sacrifice. This permits the survivors to atone for any real or fancied neglect of the deceased prior to his death. (Vernon 1970:163)

The nature of human relationships — that is, the fact that we seldom do all we feel responsible for doing in any given relationship — often produces the guilt described above, with the result that we *do* tend to overspend on funerals, sometimes encouraged by a gentle nudge from the funeral director. (See Mitford 1963)

If the expense of the funeral is a symbolic gift to the dead, an atonement for the wrongs we may have done him, the floral offerings of friends and relatives are offerings to the mourners, expressing sincere sympathy or in some cases attempting to curry favor. A photo in the *Boston Globe* several years ago depicted the start of a funeral procession in the city's North End where following the hearse there were twenty-two Cadillac flower cars full of bouquets. The deceased was the mother of an important underworld figure whose associates took the occasion as an opportunity to cement their alliances with the chief mourner. The money offerings at a Korean funeral can be used for a similar purpose, as in the case of a local government official who spent all that could be expected of one in his influential position, feeding five hundred guests from all over the province at his mother's funeral. Though the funeral expenses amounted to over $1200, his would-be allies and friends gave him over $2500 in cash as condolence money.

In the U.S., funerals for those both destitute and virtually friendless are often paid for by a charity or church organization. I remember my mother speaking of the church paying for a funeral wreath so that there would be *some* flowers at the funeral of a person who had lived virtually outside the social world. In this case it was perhaps the collective guilt of the community, as well as their genuine concern, which motivated a floral offering. A wreath should be a symbol of friendship and care, but without other wreaths to accompany it, it becomes a symbol of the social life of the deceased, one which seems in this case to have been as empty as the chapel on the day of the funeral. The number in attendance at a funeral, as well as flowers from those who cannot attend, symbolize a person's social importance. This symbol also *functions* as support for the mourners, assuring them that although one of their social relationships has been severed, many others are there to fill in some of the emptiness.

The contrast between floral and food offerings is instructive. Gifts of any kind are more appropriately luxury items than necessities — hence the designation "gift shop" for a place that sells pretty but almost invariably non-utilitarian items. The symbolism of a food offering is diluted by the fact of its utility, but flowers are pure symbol, since their only function is to look nice for a short space of time. An affluent society like our own can afford to spend lavishly on pure symbols, but in rural Korea, where the task of keeping food on the table has until quite recently been very difficult, the food offering at the altar to the deceased, financed largely through the contributions of the guests, will be consumed by either the guests themselves, the coffin bearers, or the mourners. Thus the offering is *both* symbolic and practical. Some nutritionists have estimated that for the average Korean farmer in the countryside, who normally does not buy meat for his own consumption, the pork and seafood eaten at funerals and other ritual occasions provides a vital source of protein. Also, the nutritional input comes at a time when it is most needed, during the cold winter, since most people seem to choose (if indeed it can be a choice) that season to die.[4]

The Grave and the Burial

Korean burials take place on a mountainside, usually on land owned by the lineage — a kind of huge family plot. The exact location of the grave in that area is something to be determined by a geomancer, a person trained in the understanding of the cosmic forces of *yin* and *yang*. By making certain astrological calculations and assessing the natural forces of land configuration, he is able to determine the direction in which the deceased should face when buried, as well as to choose an auspicious gravesite for the burial. Success in this venture insures the good fortune of the deceased person's family. (See Yoon 1976) Quite often, the initial burial will be regarded as temporary, and the bones will be dug up and cleaned after three years to be reburied in a permanent resting place. The coffin itself is not important, and the faster it rots the better, but the bones should be preserved — lying in their proper order — so that the geomantic forces can influence family fortunes for the better. For this reason, most graves are located on ridges on the mountainside, where adequate drainage provides for a relatively dry grave and well-preserved bones.[5]

The direction in which the corpse faces in the Korean case is calculated according to each person's own astrological coordinates, as indicated in his birth date and death date. The direction of the burial is recorded in the family genealogical record, along with the location of the grave, birth date, death date, information on the person's spouse and his/her family, and a short biographical sketch if the person held political office. With such a record, the grave can almost always be located, even if it is not marked, and the success of the geomantic calculations can, over time, be assessed.

During the burial, the chief mourners stand on top of the

coffin and tramp down the earth as it is thrown into the grave. This is a kind of final service they perform with the physical remains of the deceased and functions as a tangible involvement in the death process that helps the mourners to accept the finality of what has happened. The grave is completed by building a mound of dirt and covering it with turf. Graves are always highly visible, and not confined (in the countryside at least) to one or another particular area. In this way, the dead surround the living, keeping a vigil, and the living are reminded of their forebears and their responsibilities to carry on the traditions of those who have passed on.

After the burial, the first food offering to the transported spirit is made with the mourners bowing twice in unison and a message being read to the spirit. The funeral bier is burned near the gravesite and another wine and food offering is made to the mountain god, exhorting him to protect the grave from disturbance. The mountain ridges where people are buried are referred to as *son san* ("mountains of the elders") and, where financially possible, a keeper is employed to watch over and care for the graves.

In the American tradition, graveyards used to be located next to churches, where they were highly visible. Later practice was, however, to locate cemeteries in the outskirts of a town — out of sight and therefore less a reminder of death's presence. While gravesites do even now vary in price according to whether the view is good or not, nothing comparable to the geomantic tradition is found in burial customs in America.

Rather than the bare earth and the waiting grave that confront the Korean mourners as they approach the burial site, American custom is to cover such stark appearances with flowers and artificial grass. The mourners sometimes sit for a short graveside service but do not participate in the burial itself. Jewish practice is, however, to omit the cosmetics of the gravesite and to encourage the mourners to throw in at least the first few handfuls of dirt. Like the Korean custom, this allows physical, tangible confirmation of the reality of death and is, at the same time, service to the deceased. A study of the appearance of a Jewish cemetery will also reveal that no vault, with its function of preventing sinkage of the earth and grass above the coffin, is used. The terrain is bumpy and uneven with little or no effort at beautification. This contrasts with the American ideal in its extreme form, as illustrated by Forest Lawn Cemetery in California, which tends to look very little like a place where the dead are buried. Some call such visual euphemisms denial; others point to practicality (keeping the grass mowed is easier with non-protruding headstones); and others regard such beautifications as respect for the dead.

A close look at Utah cemeteries, where Mormons have been buried for several generations, reveals that Mormons are preferably buried facing east, all in rows, in anticipation of rising to meet Christ at His second coming. Koreans are buried in distinct, individual directions, and the contrast with Mormon burial conveys a symbolic message about the nature of religious beliefs in the two traditions. Confucianism, which is the foundation of Korean funeral practices (although there are some Buddhist elements involved), is thoroughly individual in nature — very few group meetings are held, and Confucianists owe little or no allegiance to a central authority. While Mormonism includes a belief in the individual "working out his own salvation," it is clear that his participation in communal activities such as church worship is important and that his salvation is assured only through the Savior, whom he lies in wait to greet.

Post-Funeral Mourning

Korean custom used to call for a three-year mourning period for the parents or husband and lesser lengths of time for those less closely related. The practice now is for parents or spouse to be in an official state of mourning for a full year, although in practice, men do not often behave or dress differently except that their ritual participation is curtailed. For the first thirty days after the funeral of a parent, food offerings are made every morning and night in a shrine either in the home or in a hut constructed for that purpose in the yard. When the offerings are made, mourning attire is worn. After the first thirty days, offerings are made on the first and fifteenth of each lunar month. On the anniversary of the death, a kind of second funeral is held in which another feast is prepared and the relatives and friends who attended the original funeral come again, bow and pay respects to the deceased at an altar, and express condolences to the mourners. After this occasion, the mourning clothes are burned, the shrine is dismantled, and the family makes offerings to the deceased only on special holidays and on the anniversary of his death. Such ceremonies are held in the home for four generations after a person dies, performed by the direct male descendant through the line of eldest sons. With the fifth generation, rites are held only once a year, at the graveside rather than in the home, attended by what by then is usually a large number of descendants. This graveside rite never ceases. As long as there are descendants, there are offerings of food and wine for the ancestor. In this way the generations are linked together in a never-ending chain of rites and remembrance, and detailed genealogical records are kept to insure the continuity of such ancestral rites.

Jewish custom provides a seven-day period following the burial of the deceased called *shiva*. During this time, all the mourners stay in the home of the deceased, hold daily services there, and conform to the rules of the *shiva* period, which include not wearing leather shoes, not grooming or shaving (all mirrors in the house are covered), sitting on a low stool (closer to the ground which has claimed the deceased), abstaining from work or conducting any business, and wearing clothing which was torn in the *keriah*. The requirement that ten adult men be present in order to hold the daily service means that relatives and neighbors call on the mourners continually during this time; during the latter part of the week they often provide an additional resource for listening to and consoling the mourners in their grief. *Sheloshim* is the name of the thirty-day period of mourning which includes *shiva* and during which Jewish mourners slowly begin to reenter normal life. If the deceased was a parent, however, mourning continues for a full twelve months, during which those in mourning should not take part in anything festive or joyous. The clothing torn in the *keriah* is mended or discarded only at the end of the twelve-month period.

Korean and Jewish mourning customs share the common features of responsibility for mourning based on the degree of kin relationship between the deceased and the mourner and of decreasing intensity over the set period of a year. Mourners are encouraged, in these traditions, to withdraw initially from normal activities and then gradually to return to a fully active life. During the mourning period, there are institutionally organized occasions at which support for the mourners is expressed by friends and family members, and mourners themselves are encouraged to actively express their remembrance of the dead and their grief, both verbally and through physical activities and gestures (ritual). At first glance, the American tradition is, for Mormons and others, particularly impoverished in this regard. After the funeral, we are expected to return to normal activities — nothing we wear or observe to do sets us off outwardly as being in mourning. Many widows I have known do visit the graves of their husbands on the anniversary of death, but in doing so they lack the group support and social interaction which is institutionalized in other traditions. The American Memorial Day does function as an institutional support for mourners, and some extended families make it a practice to gather on that occasion to remember their parents and other family members who have passed on. Memorial Day does, however, function to depersonalize mourning by lumping it all together — as though there is a collective attempt to get it all over with so that we need not bother again until next year.

A recent photo published in the *Boston Globe* describes an "innovation" in the American funeral industry. An enterprising funeral director in Louisiana has installed a picture window next to the driveway of his funeral home, and a man is shown leaning out the window of his automobile to sign the guest register while "viewing" the deceased, who is on display in his casket on the other side of the window pane. The caption reads, in part: "If you don't have the time or don't like the tenseness of offering sympathies to survivors, there is a new innovation. . . ." While many Jews do not sit *shiva* and many Koreans do not observe the proper mourning rites, their traditions are nonetheless preserved and practiced by a large percentage of their people and function to reaffirm religious belief, to provide for effective grief work and reintegration for mourners, and to reinforce ritually the social structure, particularly the strength of families. If the drive-in wake is an indicator of the future direction of American funeral practices, we are facing the loss of even the meager mechanisms we have left to provide socially acceptable ways of dealing with death, grief, and mourning. In addition, such practices reinforce the prevalent denial of death's reality among Americans, a denial built of fear, which causes a great deal of suffering for individuals and their families who always and finally have to confront what they have denied.

Are Mormons in America subject to the same fear and denial and, more to the point, are they left to fend for themselves, without benefit of institutional and ritual means to deal effectively with death? Beyond a strong belief in the afterlife with the reassurance that belief can bring, a casual investigation of funerals and mourning in Mormondom leaves one with the initial impression that, in the case of a death in his family, the Mormon in America is involved in only slightly more ritual than his non-Mormon neighbor. However, upon closer scrutiny, there is a ritual complex which, like Korean ancestor rites with their accompanying genealogical records and the graves of the ancestors looking down from the hillsides, serves to bind the generations together and enable the living to actively do something to preserve and extend those inter-generational ties. That complex is, of course, found in temple ceremonies, which focus most often on the dead. Temple rites allow a person in mourning to be reassured, ritually, of the continued existence of a loved one and to be reminded of the closeness between the world of the dead and that of the living. Not forcing a mourner into an active, socially demanding renewal of life, temple ceremonies nonetheless permit a person in mourning to actively engage in something he believes to be of benefit to others, thus helping him to turn away from withdrawal and grief toward an active, useful involvement. Attendance in the temple enables him to be alone in this thoughts without being lonely, and he can seek this environment, with its built-in social support, when he is most in need. Though temple worship does not normally perform such functions for the person not in mourning, for one who is trying to cope with the loss through death, Mormons temples can provide the same sort of emotional and social support as that available to the Korean or Jew in their more specialized rituals and mourning practices. The symbolic messages and the social and psychological functions of Mormon temple ceremonies are, from this point of view, very similar in structure, if not in content, to portions of other ritual complexes, most especially those associated with grief and mourning. The combination of the tradition of family prayer when a casket is closed, burial clothing of religious significance, and the symbolism and functions of temple rites, provides ritual mechanisms for coping with death beyond those available to the average non-Mormon American.

Summary

From the analysis of funeral rites and mourning customs in the context of these three traditions, it is clear that the usual behavior of those who suffer the loss of a relative or friend through death is both highly symbolic and strongly functional. Religious beliefs are illuminated symbolically in the construction and decoration of coffins, methods of burial, and the way the dead are regarded and dealt with in post-funeral rituals. Funerals are clear symbolic portrayals of the social order, and the contrast between funeral rites in two cultures, as in the comparison of Mormon-American with rural Korean funerals, can point to important differences in the ways the two societies are structured. Funeral ritual also functions to reify the prevailing social order in the minds of those who participate and observe, and to emphasize the changes in a family and/or community that occur with death. The seemingly universal tendency for people of all cultures to feel guilty or helpless or betrayed at the death of a loved one is dealt with quite effectively in institutionalized mourning customs and requirements.

Death is a universal, natural fact, but there are as many different ways to deal with it as there are cultural traditions among mankind. It is hoped that this rudimentary analysis of three of these ways will illustrate the wealth of information to be gained through the study of funerals and mourning and also provide the reader with further insight into what his own ritual tradition has to offer him.

NOTES

1. In Mormondom, the succession of rites of passage for males includes the blessing and naming of newborns, baptism, ordination to Aaronic and Melchizedek Priesthood, the temple endowment, missionary service, marriage, and the funeral.

2. This idea can be attributed to Jung and his "collective unconscious," as quoted in Turner 1967:36.

3. My rapport with people in the village where I did my fieldwork suffered on one occasion when I should have attended a funeral and did not. An opportunity to symbolize my membership in the community passed, and my absence was a sign of my admitted outsider's status.

4. Of the fifteen deaths which occurred during my stay in the village, fourteen took place in the winter or early spring. The one exception was the funeral of a young man who died in a city hospital.

5. The story is told of a man who hired a geomancer to find a good grave site (current fees for finding, not purchasing, a very good site are in excess of $500). The geomancer came upon what he regarded as a tremendously good site, saying that the fourth generation descendants of the person buried there would become fabulously successful. The client, not willing to wait for his descendants to benefit, dug up the bones of his great-grandfather and had them reinterred in the auspicious site. He of course became wealthy and famous.

BIBLIOGRAPHY

Em Mwun-ho. 1974. *Taykacengpokam* (A Family Handbook). Seoul: Hankwuk Tose Mwunhawasa.

Faulkner, William. 1930. *As I Lay Dying*. New York: Jonathan Cape: Harrison Smith.

Hinton, John. 1976. "Speaking of Death with the Dying" in *Death: Current Perspectives*. Edwin S. Shneidman, ed. Palo Alto: Mayfield Publishing Co., pp. 303-314.

Kübler-Ross, Elisabeth. 1969. *On Death and Dying*. New York: Macmillan Publishing Co.

Lamm, Maurice. 1969. *The Jewish Way in Death and Mourning*. New York: Jonathan David Publishers.

Leach, Edmund. 1976. *Culture and Communication*. New York: Cambridge University Press.

Lee Kwang-kyu. 1975. *A Structural Analysis of the Korean Family* (in Korean with some chapters in English). Seoul: Ilcisa.

Levi-Strauss, Claude. 1963. *Structural Anthropology*. Trans. C. Jacobson and B. G. Schoept. New York: Basic Books.

Malinowski, Bronislaw. 1948. *Magic, Science and Religion*. New York: Doubleday Anchor Books.

Mitford, Jessica. 1963. *The American Way of Death*. New York: Simon and Schuster.

Turner, Victor. 1967. *The Forest of Symbols*. Ithaca: Cornell University Press.

Van Gennep, Arnold. 1960. *The Rites of Passage*. Chicago: University of Chicago Press. (First published in 1908)

Vernon, Glen M. 1970. *The Sociology of Death*. New York: Ronald Press.

Yoon, Hong-key. 1976. *Geomantic Relationships Between Nature and Culture in Korea*. Taipei: The Orient Cultural Service. (Vol. 80 of Asian Folklore and Social Life Monographs)

Death and Dying in the Middle East

2

Sami A. Hanna

Death and dying are universal realities for all creations in every country and cultural area. What makes death and dying so interesting is that its treatment varies from one country to another and from one culture to another. For example, if we take Europe as a whole, its people meet death and behave differently from the people of the Middle East.

We know something about the people of the Middle East, but we are not well acquainted with certain important cultural patterns of that area. When we go as Americans or Europeans, we focus our attention on movements, tourist attractions, etc., but we seldom care to see or investigate how the Middle Eastern people respond to death and dying.

Since this area is predominantly Muslim, our attention is focused on the attitudes and beliefs of the people of this faith. Most examples presented are derived from the Holy Qur'ān, the *Hadith,* and other Islamic texts. Other basic sources are *Hughes' Dictionary of Islam,* the *Encyclopedia of Islam,* and my own personal experiences and observations. I have relied on these latter books through this presentation, but I have not sought to cite page numbers in every instance, except when quoting from passages in the Qur'ān.

First, however, I would like to share with you my impressions, as a Middle Easterner, of my first experience with an American funeral, which took place in Salt Lake City. The father of one of my very close friends died. I wanted, of course, to express my condolences to him but learned that such condolences are expressed in a mortuary. I located the mortuary and went there. I found myself in a large building with several rooms, each of which was reserved for a deceased person. A man ushered me into one of the rooms. When I entered and approached the family, I was utterly shocked. The family was standing in line, friends were also standing in line, so I stood in line. When my turn came, I expressed my sympathy to my friend. However, what was even more shocking to me was the spirit in which the family received me. "Look how nice he is. Doesn't he look wonderful?" These and other things were said in a joyful spirit. To be honest, I expected to see the family of the deceased crying and screaming as in the Middle Eastern culture. But that was not the case. After viewing the deceased in his half-open casket, I returned home wondering how death in America, at least in this Mormon setting, could be received with such joy and happiness. When I asked my friend about this attitude, I was told that death is a transition — a bridge to a happy and everlasting life in heaven.

Such a belief caused me to ponder and to ask myself why we receive death completely differently in the Middle East than in the West? Why do we cry and scream for at least a year? Why do men wear black ties and women black garments? Why do we abstain from everything sweet, from food, from even listening to the radio? Why do the neighbors turn off their radios as a token of sympathy? Why do we remain in mourning for at least forty days?

Death Among Muslims

Death in Arabic is *Mawt; Wafāt*. It is clearly taught in the Qur'ān, which is read by several hundred million Muslims all over the globe, that "The hour of death is fixed for every living creature.'' There are many references in the Holy Qur'ān about death. For example, in Sūra xvi. 63, we find that:

> If God were to punish men for their wrongdoing, He would not leave on the earth a single living creature; but he respites them until a stated time; and when their time comes they cannot delay it an hour, nor can they hasten it.

Also in Sūra iii. 82:

> Every soul must taste death, and he shall only be paid his hire on the day of resurrection.

Furthermore, in Sūra 1. 17 we learn that death is not a single thing:

> The agony of death shall come in truth, that is what thou didst shun.

According to the Traditions, as depicted by Hughes' account,[1] Muhammed was taught that it is sinful to wish for death:

> ''Wish not for death, not even if thou art a doer of good works, for peradventure thou mayest increase them with an increase [of life]. . . . Not even if thou art a sinner, for which increase of life thou mayest obtain God's pardon.''

According to Islamic tradition, one day the Prophet said:

> Whosoever loves to meet God, God will love to meet him, and whosoever dislikes to meet God, God will dislike to meet him. Then ᶜĀyishah said:
>
> ''Truly we all dislike death and consider it a great affliction.'' The Prophet replied:
>
> ''Thou dost not understand me. When death comes near a believer, God gives him a spirit of resignation, and so it is that there is nothing which a believer likes so much as death.''

An interesting story about death is narrated by Al-Barā' ibn ᶜĀzib, one of the companions of the Prophet:

I came out with the Prophet at the funeral of one of the assistants, and we arrived just at the grave, before they had interred the body, and the Prophet sat down, and we sat around him with our heads down, and were so silent that you might say that birds were sitting upon our heads. And there was a stick in the Prophet's hand with which he kept striking the ground. Then he raised his head and said twice or thrice to his companions,

"Seek the protection of God from the punishments of the grave."

After that he said, "Verily, when a Muslim separateth from the world and bringeth his soul to futurity, angels descend to him from the celestial regions, whose faces are white. You might say their faces are the sun, and they have a shroud of the shrouds of paradise, and perfumes therefrom. So they sit apart from the deceased, as far as the eyes can see, after which the 'Angel of Death' [Malāku'l-Mawt] comes to the deceased and sits at his head and says, 'O pure soul, come forth to God's pardon and pleasure.'

"Then the soul comes out, issuing like water from a bag, and the Angel of Death takes it; and when he takes it, the angels do not allow it to remain in his hands for the twinkling of an eye. But when the Angel of Death has taken the soul of a servant of God, he resigns it to his assistants, in whose hands is a shroud, and they put it into the shroud with perfumes, and a fragrance issues from the soul like the smell of the best musk that is to be found on the face of the earth.

"Then the angels carry it upwards, and they do not pass by any concourse of angels who say, 'What is this pure soul and who is the owner of it?'

"And they say, 'Such a one, the son of such a one,' calling him by the best names by which he was known in the world, till they reach the lowest region of heaven with him. And the angels ask the door to be opened for him, which is done.

"Then angels follow it through each heaven, the angel of one heaven to those of the next, and so on till it reaches the seventh heaven, when God says, 'Write the name of my servant in ᶜĪlliyūn, and return him towards the earth, that is, to his body which is buried in the earth, because I have created man from earth and return him to it, and will bring him out from it again as I brought him out at first.'

"Then the souls are returned into their bodies, when two angels [Munkar and Nakir] come to the dead man and cause him to sit up, and say to him, 'Who is the Lord?'

"He replies, 'My Lord is God.'

"Then they say, 'What is thy religion?'

"He says, 'Islām.'

"Then they say, 'What is this man who is sent to you?' (i.e., the Prophet)

"He says, 'He is the Prophet of God.'

"Then they say, 'What is your proof of his mission?'

"He says, 'I read the book of God and believed in it, and I proved it to be true.'

"Then a voice calls out from the celestial regions, 'My servant hath spoken true, therefore throw for him a bed from Paradise, and dress him in clothes from Paradise,[2] and open a door for him towards Paradise.'

"Then peace and perfumes come for him from Paradise, and his grave is enlarged for him as far as the eye can see. Then a man with a beautiful face comes to him, elegantly dressed and perfumed, and he says, 'Be joyful in that which hath made thee so; this is the day which was promised thee.'

"Then the dead person says to him, 'Who art thou, for thy face is perfectly beautiful.'

"And the man replies, 'I am thy good deeds.'

"Then the dead person cries out, 'O Lord, hasten the resurrection for my sake!'

"But," continued the Prophet, "when an infidel dies and is about to pass from the world and bring his soul to futurity, *black-faced angels*[3] come down to him and with them sackcloths. Then they sit from the dead as far as the eye can see, after which the Angel of Death comes in order to sit at his head and says,

" 'O impure soul! Come forth to the wrath of God.'

"Then the soul is disturbed in the infidel's body. Then the Angel of Death draws it out as hot spit is drawn out of wet wool.

"Then the Angel of Death takes the soul of the infidel, and having taken it, the angels do not allow it to remain with him even for the twinkling of an eye, but they take it in the sackcloth, and a disagreeable smell issues from the soul, like that of the most fetid carcass that can be met with upon the face of the earth.

"Then the angels carry it upwards and do not pass by any assembly of angels who do not ask whose filthy soul is this. They answer such an one, the son of such an one, and they mention him by the worst names that he bore in the world, till they arrive with it at the lowest heaven, and call the door to be opened, but it cannot be done."

Then the Prophet repeated this verse: "The doors of the celestial regions shall not be opened for them, nor shall they enter into Paradise till a camel passes through the eye of a needle.[4]

"Then God says, 'Write his history in *Sijjīn*,' which is the lowest earth; then his soul is thrown down with violence."

Afterwards the Prophet repeated this verse: "Unite no partner with God, for whoever uniteth gods with God is like that which falleth from on high, and the birds snatch it away, or the wind wafteth it to a distant place.

"Then his soul is replaced in his body, and two angels [*Munkar* and *Nakir*] come to him and set him up, and say,

" 'Who is thy Lord?'

"He says, 'Alas! Alas! I do not know.'

"Then they say, 'What is thy religion?'

"He says, 'Alas, alas! I do not know.'

"And they say to him, 'What is the condition of the man who is sent down to you?'

"He says, 'Alas, alas! I do not know.'

"Then a voice comes from above saying, 'He lieth; therefore spread a bed of fire for him and open a door for him towards hell.'

"Then the heat and hot winds of hell come to him, and his grave is made tight upon him, so as to squeeze his ribs. And a man with a hideous countenance comes to him shockingly dressed, of a vile smell, and he says, 'Be joyful in that which maketh thee miserable; this is the day that was promised thee.'

"Then the dead man says, 'Who art thou? Thy face is hideous and brings wickedness.'

"He says, 'I am thy impure actions.'

"Then the dead person says, 'O Lord, delay the resurrection on my account!' "

The ceremonies attending the death of a Muslim are described by Jāfir Sharīf in Herklot's *Qānūn-i-Islām*, "Islamic Law" page 80. Four or five days before a sick man's dissolution, he makes his will in favor of his son or any other person in the presence of two or more witnesses and either delivers this will to others or retains it. In it he likewise appoints his executor. When he is about to expire, any learned reader of the Qur'ān is sent for and requested to repeat, with a loud voice, "*Sūrat Yā Sīn*" (or

Chapter xxxvi in the Qur'ān), in order that the spirit of the man, by the hearing of its sound, may experience an easy concentration. It is said that when the spirit was commanded to enter the body of Adam, the soul looked into it once and observed that it was a bad and dark place and unworthy of its presence. Then the Just and Most Holy God illuminated the body of Adam with "lamps of light" and commanded the spirit to re-enter. It went in a second time, beheld the light, saw the whole dwelling and said, "There is no pleasing sound here for me to listen to." It is generally understood from the best works of the mystics of the East that it was because of this circumstance that the Almighty created music. The Holy Spirit, on hearing the sound of this music, became so delighted that it entered Adam's body.

Commentators on the Qur'ān and expositors of the Traditions and divines have written that the sound resembled that produced by the repeating of the *Sūrat Yā Sīn;* it is therefore advisable to read at the hour of death this chapter from the Qur'ān for tranquilizing the soul.

The *Kalimatu 'sh-shahāda* (the [creed]) is also read with an audible voice by those present. They do not require the patient to read it himself, since at that time he is in a state of distress and not in a fit state of mind to repeat the *Kalimah*.

Most people lie insensible and cannot even speak, but the pious retain their mental faculties and converse till the very end. There is a most serious religious rule amongst Muslims that if there is a desire for the dying person to repeat the *Kalimah,* and the sick man expires without being able to do so, his faith is considered dubious, and the man who directed him to repeat the *Kalimah* incurs guilt. It is therefore best that those sitting with the dying person read it, in hopes that the sick man, hearing the sound of it, may bring it to his recollection and repeat it either aloud or in his own mind. Usually when a person is on the point of death, someone pours *sharbat,*[5] made of sugar and water, down his throat to facilitate the exit of the vital spark, and someone procures the holy water of the Zamzam well at Mecca.[6]

The moment the spirit has fled, the mouth is closed, because it would present a disagreeable spectacle. The two great toes are brought in contact and fastened with a thin strip of cloth to keep the legs together. Perfumes[7] are burned near the corpse. If the individual died in the evening, the shrouding and burial take place before midnight; if he died at a later hour, he is buried early the next morning. The sooner the sepulchral rites are performed, the better; for it is not proper to keep a corpse long in the house.[8] For this reason the Prophet said that the sooner a good man is buried, the more quickly he will reach heaven. If a bad man, he should be speedily buried so that his unhappy lot will not fall upon others in the house, and so that the relatives of the deceased may not, by holding the corpse, weep too much or go without food.[9]

There are male and female washers[10] who are hired to wash and shroud the corpse. Sometimes, however, the relatives do it themselves. They dig a hole in the earth to contain the water used in the washing and to keep it from spreading over a large surface, as some men and women consider it bad to tread on such water. Some women who are particular in these matters are afraid even to venture near the place where the body has been washed. The corpse is placed on a bed, a country cot, a plank, or on straw then stripped and laid on its back with its head to the east and feet to the west. The washers cover it with a cloth that reaches, for a man, from the navel to the calves of the legs, or for a woman, from the chest to the feet. They wash the corpse with warm or cold water, raising the body gently and rubbing the abdomen four or five times. Then they pour plenty of water on the corpse and wash off all the dirt and filth with soap, using flocks of cotton or cloth. Next they wash the sides of the body, then the back and the rest of the body, gently, because life has just departed and the body is still warm and sensitive to pain. The body is cleaned well so that no offensive smell remains. The washers never throw water into the nostrils or mouth but clean them with wicks of cloth or cotton. Then they perform *wuḍū'k*[11] for the person; they wash his mouth, and arms to the elbows; they make *masaḥ* on his head and they throw water on his feet — these actions constituting the four parts of the ceremony. They then put some camphor with water into a new large earthen pot and with another new earthen pot they take out water and pour it on the body three times: first from the head to the feet, then from the right shoulder to the feet, finally from the left shoulder to the feet. Every time a pot of water is poured the

Kalimatu 'sh-shāda (the words of testimony) is repeated: "*Ash-hahadu an lā illa Allāh* which means "I testify that there is no deity but God"), either by the person washing or someone else. After the body is bathed and wiped dry with a new piece of cloth, it is placed in the shrouds.

The shrouds consist of three pieces of cloth for a man and five for a woman. The shroud for men is a special set of burial clothes: first, a *lungi* or *izār*[12] that reaches from the navel to the knees or ankle joints; second, a *qamīṣ* or *kurta* or *alfā,*[13] that hangs from the neck to the knees or ankles; third, a *lifāfah*[14] or sheet that extends above the head to below the feet. Women have two additional pieces of cloth: a *sīnah-band* or breast-band, that extends from the armpits to just above the ankle joints; the other a *daminī* which encircles the head once and has two ends dangling on each side.

Having placed the shrouds on a new mat and fumigated them with the smoke of perfumes, the *lifāfah* is spread first on the mat, over it the *lungī* or *izār,* and above that the *qamīṣ* and on that the *sīnah-band,* if it is a woman. The *daminī* is kept separate and tied on afterwards. The corpse must be carefully brought from the place it was bathed and laid on the shrouds.

Surmah is applied to the eyes with a tent made of rolled up paper with a ring or with a *pice*. Camphor is applied in seven places: on the forehead including the nose, on the palms of the hands, on the knees, and on the great toes. Then the different shrouds are put on properly, one after another as they lay. The color of the shroud is to be white; no other is admissible. It is of no consequence if a colored cloth is spread over the bier. After the funeral or after the fortieth day, this cloth is given to the faqir[15] who resides in the burying-ground or to any other person deserving of charity. Before shrouding the body, the family tears shreds from the clothes. After shrouding is completed, these shreds are tied on the body: one band above the head, a second below the feet, and a third about the chest, leaving six or seven fingers' breadth of cloth above the head and below the feet to permit the ends to be fastened. In the case of a deceased female, if relatives are present, they undo the cloth of the head to expose the face and ask the dead person, in the presence of two witnesses, to remit the dowry which had been given her. However, it is preferable that this dowry be remitted while the person is still alive.

If the mother of the deceased is present, she says, "The milk with which I suckled thee I freely bestow on thee"; but this is primarily a custom in India. It is neither enjoined in books of theology nor by the law of Islam. Finally the family places a flower-sheet or wreath of flowers on the corpse.[16]

Views of the Hereafter

Arthur Jefrey, an authority on Islām, gives a number of accounts regarding death and the hereafter. Jefrey observes that "Whosoever has a loving desire to meet with Allāh is one whom Allāh has a loving desire to meet."[17] He states that by meeting with Allāh (he means death), the true believer is in such a state that he cannot be responsible for his faith; thus, he will be given the good news that Allāh is well pleased with him and will grant him His Paradise. To die will be more desirable to the true believer than to live. After meeting him, Allāh will pour out upon him His grace and give bountifully of His gifts.

Jefrey also reports that the Prophet once said that "He who is disinclined to meet with Allāh is one whom Allāh is disinclined to meet." In other words, when an unbeliever thinks of the punishment that has been prepared for him, he weeps for his doom and is disinclined to die, so Allāh is disinclined to meet with him. The meaning of "disinclined" when used in reference to Allāh's relations with a man is that Allāh puts the man far from His mercy, and wills his punishment. This has nothing to do with painful emotions, the attribution of which to Allāh — exalted be He — would not be fitting.

There is another view which says that the meaning of the Tradition is not that one's loving desire to meet with Allāh is the cause of Allāh's loving desire to meet with him, nor that one's disinclination is the cause of His disinclination. The Tradition is intended to describe clearly those people who desire to meet with Allāh when Allāh desires to meet with them. This is all he says, and its purport obviously is that "loving desire" is an attribute of Allāh, and a human's loving desire for his Lord springs from it and is a reflection, like the reflection of water on a wall. Islamic tradition supports the idea that "When Allāh loves a man He keeps him busy with himself." That His loving them precedes their loving Him is indicated in the Qur'ān. When Muhammed made the statement above, people responded, "But, O Apostle of Allāh, we are all disinclined to die." He answered: "That is not disinclination. Whenever a believer comes to die a messenger of good tidings (*bashīr*)[18] will appear, bringing to him from Allāh — exalted be He — news of the good to which he is going, so there will be nothing for which he has greater loving desire than for the meeting with Allāh — exalted be He — and Allāh will have a loving desire to meet with him. But when an iniquitous man — or some related that he said, an unbeliever — comes to die, a messenger of ill tidings (*nadhīr*) will appear, bringing him news of the evil that awaits him, so he will be disinclined to meet with Allāh, and Allāh disinclined to meet with him.

On another occasion the Prophet said:

> Relate [religious traditions] from the Children of Israel. There is no crime in that, for they are a people among whom marvelous things have happened.

Then he himself began to relate and said:

> Once there was a group of the Children of Israel who as they were walking along came presently to a grave-yard. They said, "Let us set ourselves to prayer, and then make supplication to our Lord, and maybe he will allow one of the dead to come forth to inform us about dying."
>
> So they set themselves to prayer and made supplication to their Lord, and while they were engaged in so doing a dark mulatto raised his head out of one of the graves, saying, "Ho! You there! What do you want? By Allāh, though I died ninety years ago the bitterness of dying[19] has not left me till this moment. Make supplication to Allāh for me that he let me be again as I was (among the living)."

As for dying, he said, "For a true believer the distress and anxiety of dying are equivalent to that from three hundred strokes."

The Prophet spoke clearly about the distress and bitterness of dying as a word of wholesome advice to his community. He hoped that they might prepare themselves for dying and bear with patient endurance (*ṣabr*) the distresses of this world; for endurance of the distresses of this world is easier than to endure the distress of dying, and the distress of dying belongs to the torments of the Hereafter, and the torments of the afterlife are more severe than the torments of this life.

Muhammed was once asked by a Muslim:

> "What have you done about giving Him His due?"
> "What Allāh has willed," answered the Prophet, "And do you know death?"
> "Yes," answered he.
> "Then what have you done in preparation for it?" asked the Prophet.
> "What Allāh has willed," answered he.
> So the Prophet said, "Go and put in practice what that involves, then come and I will teach you of the wonders of learning."
> Then he said, "When the light of Islām enters the heart it becomes at ease and is enlarged." Someone asked, "And is there any [outward] sign of that?" To which he answered:
> "Yes! A withdrawing from the abode of the illusory, a coming back to the abode of the eternal, and a making preparation for death before it comes upon one."

Ja^{c}Far b. Burqān has related from Maymūn B. Mihrān that the Prophet said to a man, as he was exhorting him:

> Lay hands on the opportunity for five things before five: on your youth before you become decrepit; on your health before you become sick; on your leisure before you become busily occupied; on your wealth before you become poor; and on your life before you die.

From these five precepts a man can gather much wisdom; for a man is capable of works during his youth of which he is incapable in the years of his old age. If a youth becomes accustomed to doing deeds of disobedience, he cannot refrain from them in his later years. So a youth in the period of his youthfulness ought to become accustomed to doing good deeds and then doing good deeds will be easy for him when he becomes old. Likewise, a healthy person can carry effectively through matters which concern his property or his person; therefore, a healthy person ought to seize the opportunity his health gives him to be diligent in using his property and his body for doing deeds of obedience. "On your leisure before you are busily occupied," means that by night one is at leisure but by day is busily occupied, therefore one ought to say prayers at night during the period of his leisure and fast by day. When he said: "On your life before you die," he means that so long as man is alive he is capable of works, but when he is dead there is an end to his works. Therefore, a true believer ought not to squander his days, which pass so quickly, but should seize the opportunity of such days as remain to him.

ᶜAli reported that Muhammed saw the Angel of Death at the head of a man of the Anṣār, so the Prophet said to him:

> "Be gentle with my friend, for he is a true believer."
>
> He answered: "Be of good cheer, O Muhammed, for I am gentle with every true believer. By Allāh, O Muhammed, if any of the family starts screaming when I am taking a man's spirit, I say, What is this screaming? By Allāh, we are doing him no injustice. We have not come before his time. We have not accelerated his fate, so what sin are we committing in taking him? If you are well pleased with what Allāh has done you will receive your reward, but if you are displeased or sore afflicted [by it], you are committing sin and being rebellious. You have no cause for discontent with us, and we are going to return for you, so let him who will beware, beware, for there are no dwellers whether in hair tents or in villages, whether on land or on sea, but we examine their faces five times daily and at night, so that I know them both small and great, know them individually. By Allāh, O Muhammed, did I desire to take the spirit of a gnat I could not do it till Allāh gave me commandment to take it."

It is related that the Apostle of Allāh said: "Did the animals [i.e. domesticated beasts] know what you know about dying you would never eat fat meat."[20]

It is recorded that Abu Ḥāmid al-Laffāf said:

> One who reminds himself frequently of death gains three precious things, viz., an urge to speedy repentance, a contentment with his daily provision, and a liveliness in

> worship, whereas one who is forgetful of death will be punished for three things, for postponing repentance, for not being content with a sufficiency, and for laziness in [matters of] worship.

It is recorded in Muslim sources that Jesus used to raise the dead by Allāh's permission. Some of the unbelievers said to him:

> "You have been raising to life those who had but recently died and who maybe were not quite dead. Raise to life for us someone who died in ancient times."
>
> He said to them: "Choose whomsoever you will."
>
> They replied: "Raise for us Shem, Noah's son."
>
> So he went to Shem's grave, prayed a prayer of two *rakᶜas,* and made supplication to Allāh — exalted be He — whereupon Allāh raised to life Shem the son of Noah, and lo, his head and beard had gone white.
>
> They said: "What is this? Folks used not to go grey in your time."
>
> He said: "I heard the summons, and I thought it was the resurrection, so out of fear my head and my beard went white."
>
> Someone asked: "How long have you been dead?" and he answered, "Four thousand years, yet the anguish of dying[21] has not left me."

One Muslim authority has observed:

> Blessed is he to whom Allāh gives provision of understanding, rouses from the slumber of heedlessness, and leads to ponder over the matter of his end. Let us, therefore, ask Allāh to appoint us a good ending, to grant us an ending that is accompanied by a message of good tidings, for there is a message of good tidings from Allāh — exalted be He — for the true believer when death comes to him, and it is the words of the Most High.
>
> Verily, those who have said, "Our Lord is Allāh," and then have kept the straight course, on them will the angels descend [saying]: "Fear not! Grieve not! But rejoice in good tidings of the Garden which ye have been promised."
>
> By keeping the straight course he means believing in Allāh and in His Apostle, and standing firm in the faith, though others say that it means performing the required duties and avoiding things forbidden.

In Islām the message of good tidings at death has five aspects:

1. The first is for believers in general, who receive the message: "Fear not that the punishment will be everlasting," or, you will not remain in torment forever because the Prophet and righteous persons will intercede for you. "Grieve not lest you miss the reward, but rejoice in good tidings of the Garden," that you will assuredly go to Paradise.

2. Sincere devotees (*al-mukhliṣūn*)[22] receive the message: "Fear not that your works will be rejected, for your works are accepted; grieve not about things you may have done subsequent to your repentance."

3. Penitents receive the message: "Fear not about your sins, for they have been forgiven you, and grieve not that you may miss the reward because of anything you may have done subsequent to your repentance."

4. Ascetics (*Zuhhād*) receive the message: "Fear not the assembling and the accounting [at Judgment], and grieve not about there being any dimunition in your doubled reward, but rejoice in the good tidings that you go to Paradise without any accounting and without [having to go to Gehenna for] any torment."

5. Theologians (ᶜulāma) who teach the people, if they teach them well and live in accordance with their own teaching, will receive the message: "Fear not the terrors of the Day of Judgment; grieve not, for He will recompense you for what you have wrought, and rejoice in good tidings of the Garden, which is for you and for those who imitate your example."

Blessed is he whose ending is accompanied by a message of good tidings, for there will be such a message of good tidings only for such as have been true believers and whose works have been good. To such the angels will descend (at death), and they will say to the angels:

> Who are ye? Never have we seen faces more beautiful, nor [smelled] an odor more pleasant than yours.

They will say:

> We are your friends (awliyā),[23] i.e., your guardians who used to write down your deeds during your earthly life, but now we are to be your awliyā in the after life.

Man was created for death. There is no running away from it. Thus Allāh has said: "Flight will not benefit you at all if you are fleeing from death or being killed." So it is incumbent on each Muslim to make preparation for death before it comes. Allāh has said: "Then wish for death if ye are those who speak truth." But they will never wish for it because of what their hands have sent forward.

Allāh here makes it clear that the one who speaks truth desires death, but the false speaker flees from death because of the evil of his works. The truth-speaking believer has made preparation for death, so he wishes for it, yearning for his Lord.

It is related that there is no soul, innocent or wicked, to which death is not a good thing. If it is innocent Allāh has said, "What is with Allāh is a good thing for the innocent," and if it is wicked Allāh has said, "We respite them only that they may increase in guilt, and for them is humiliating punishment."

The Torment and Distress of the Tomb

Al'Khalīl b. Aḥmad has reported:

> We went out with the Apostle of Allāh [to join] the funeral procession on a man from the *Ansar*.[24] When we came to the grave it was not yet dug [completely], so the Prophet sat down, and we also sat around about him, and it was as though the birds were over our heads. In his hand was a rod with which he kept digging in the ground.
>
> Presently he raised his head and said: "Seek refuge with Allāh from the torment of the tomb."
>
> This he said twice or thrice, and then went on: "When a man who is a true believer is drawing near to the next world and is about to be cut off from this world, there descend to him angels whose faces are white as the sun, bringing with them a shroud from Paradise and celestial aromatics, and take a seat at his head and say, 'O thou tranquil soul, come forth to Allāh's favour and forgiveness.'
>
> "Then," said the Prophet, "it comes forth, flowing as easily as a drop from a water-skin, whereupon [those angels] take it, not leaving it in his hand more than the twinkling of an eye ere they take it, [wrap it] in the aforementioned shroud and aromatics so that the odor from it is more redolent than

the finest musk to be found on the face of the earth, and mount up with it.

"There is not a single angel group whom they pass [as they mount upwards] but asks, 'What sweet-smelling spirit is this?'

"And they reply, 'This is the spirit of so-and-so,' using the finest names for him. Anon they come with it to the gate of the lowest heaven and ask that it be opened for it. It is opened to them and the chief personages in each heaven receive it and accompany it to that which lies beyond it, till finally they arrive with it at the seventh heaven. There Allāh says, 'Write its record in ᶜIlliyūn[25] and return it to the earth from which I created men, into which I make them return, and out of which I shall bring them a second time.' (Sūra, xx, 55/57)

"The spirit is then returned to its body, whereupon two angels[26] come to it and ask it, 'Who is the Lord?'

"It replies, 'Allāh is my Lord.'

"They ask, 'And what is your religion?'

" 'Islām is my religion,' it replies.

"Then they say, 'And what say you about this man who was sent [on a mission] among you?'

"And it answers, 'He is the Apostle of Allāh.'

"They ask, 'What works have you?'

"And it answers, 'I have read Allāh's Book, believed it, and in it put my trust.'

"Then a herald will call: 'He has believed My servant (i.e. Muhammed). Spread for him a bed (firāsh) from the Garden. Clothe him in a celestial garment, open for him a door giving on the Garden through which may come to him its breezes and its aroma, and expand his grave for him as far as eye can reach.'

"Then there approaches him a sweet-smelling man of handsome countenance, who says to him: 'Good tidings of that which please you. This is your day that you were promised.'

"He will ask, 'And who are you?'

"To which the answer will come, 'I am your pious works.' Then [the deceased] will say: 'O Lord, bring on the hour that I may be again with my family and my servants.' "

The Prophet continued: "But when an unbeliever is drawing near to the next world and being cut off from this world, there descends to him from heaven angels whose faces are black, bringing with them hair-cloth, and take their seats just within his vision. Then the Angel of Death arrives, takes a seat at his head and says, 'O thou pernicious soul, come forth to Allāh's discontent and wrath.' Thereupon his soul is scattered through all his members and [the angel] drags it forth like the dragging of an iron spit through moist wool, tearing the veins and the sinews. Thus he takes it, but it is not in his hand more than the twinkling of an eye ere [those angels] take it, put it in the hair-cloth where the odor from it is like the stench of a decomposing carcass.

"They mount up with it, and there is not a single angel group whom they pass but asks, 'What impure spirit is this?'

"They reply, 'This is the spirit of So-and-so,' using the least worthy name for him. Anon they come with it to the gate of the lowest heaven and ask that it be opened for it, but it is not opened."

At this point the Apostle of Allāh recited this verse (vii 40/38):

"The gates of heaven will not be opened for them, nor will they enter the Garden till a camel passes through a needle's eye.

"[He continued,] Then Allāh will say, 'Write this record in *sijjīn*,[27] then let his spirit be thrown out.' "

At this point [the Prophet] recited (xxii, 31/32):

"He who associates anything with Allāh will be as though he fell from the sky and the birds snatched him away and the winds blew him to some remote place."

"So his spirit is returned to his body, whereupon two angels come and sit by him. They ask him, 'Who is your Lord?' and he replies, 'Alas, I know not.'

"They ask him, 'And what is your religion?' to which he again replies, 'Alas! I know not.'

"They ask, 'Well, what do you say about this man who was sent [on a mission] among you?' But again he replies, 'Alas! I know not.'

"Thereupon a herald cries from heaven: 'He has given my servant [Muhammed] the lie. Spread for him a bed from the fire, clothe him in fire, open for him a door giving on the fire, through which its heat and smoke may enter to him and contract his grave so that his ribs pile on one another.'

"Then there approaches him a man, ugly of countenance, ill dressed and foul smelling, who says to him, 'Re-

> ceive tidings of that which will grieve you. This is your day that you were promised.'
>
> "He will ask, 'And who are you?' to which [the man] will reply, 'I am your evil deeds,' whereat he will say, 'O Lord, let not the hour arrive. O Lord, let not the hour arrive.' "

The Apostle of Allāh also said:

> "When a true believer draws near his end angels come to him with a silk cloth in which are musk and bundles of sweet basil. His spirit comes forth as easily as a hair from a batch of dough, and hears the words:
>
> " 'O tranquil soul, return to your Lord, well-pleasing and well-pleased. [Go on] to the mercy and favor of Allāh — exalted be He.'
>
> "When his spirit has been drawn forth and placed in the musk and sweet basil, the silk cloth is folded and sent with it to *ᶜIllyūn*.
>
> "As for the unbeliever, when he draws near his end, angels come to him with a cloth of hair in which are coals of fire. His spirit is painfully dragged out, and hears the words,
>
> " 'O thou pernicious soul, come forth displeased and displeasing. [Go on] to Allāh's contempt and punishment.' When his spirit has been drawn forth and placed in those coals, which hiss like boiling kettles, the cloth is folded over and sent with it to *Sijjīn*."

When a true believer is placed in his grave, the grave is expanded for him seventy cubits, strewn with sweet basil, and hung with silk. If he should be one who has memorized somewhat of the Qur'ān, the light of that will suffice him, but should he have nothing (of the Qur'ān) memorized, a light equivalent to that of the sun will be put in his grave, and he himself will be like a sleeping bird who will not be wakened save by her best beloved.

At this point I feel safe in concluding that Islām in the Middle East gives more attention to death than Christianity. The aforementioned details show clearly that in Islām afterlife for good men is something to look forward to. It depicts both spiritual and material life. Conversely, Christianity generally emphasizes afterlife more than being in the world.

Death in the Days of the Pharaohs

We have now covered Islamic concepts of death and dying; let us briefly present other rites of minority groups in the Middle East.

What about Pre-Islamic Egyptian beliefs and practices concerning death? Let us go back to the days of the pharaohs of ancient Egypt. According to the oldest Egyptian beliefs, the gods also were subject to age and could die. The body was preserved so that the soul would not also die as a result of the dismemberment of the body. Legend has it that the gods Herus and Anubis cared for the dead body of Osiris, an Egyptian deity; and likewise a dead person would live on only if friends and relatives did for him just what Herus and Anubis did for the body of Osiris.

Osiris reigned in the world of the dead over the *ka* or soul of the dead. Each Egyptian burial was made out to be an exact duplicate of the god-burial. Every dead person was identified with Osiris and bore his name (the famous papyrus of Ani often mentions the dead scribe as "Osiris-Ani"). Further at Sais, the suffering of Osiris was enacted yearly and images of Osiris were filled with grain and placed with the dead person as symbols of fertility and eternal life.

Much of the Egyptian religious beliefs would show up in either culture in modified form but with a common theme as their basis. Even as late as in Egyptian Christianity, some forms are still easily identified.[28]

In ancient Egyptian religion when a pharaoh came to the throne, the first thing he planned was his tomb. Like King Tut, whose funerary remains are moving around the United States these days, the body was mummified because the Egyptians wanted the body to still be alive in the tomb. The king's soul, of course, did not die at all but moved around in heaven — like a solar boat.

In Egypt, one finds three big jars in every tomb of any pharaoh: one for his heart, one for his intestines, and one for other things. His whole body was mummified and wrapped so that he looked exactly as if he were alive. The rituals differed but the king was taken through corridors, surrounded by high priests and a variety of elaborate things, and given the best burial a man could see.

As the pharaohs disappeared in Egyptian history, they were replaced by descendants of other ancient Egyptians called the Copts. The Copts, or Christians of Egypt, have developed different burial customs. I have had personal experience with many of these. If a Christian dies in the Middle East, he is kept only until the undertaker arrives and takes care of the body. As in Jewish customs of burial, the deceased must be buried immediately. There must be no waiting. The body cannot even stay overnight.[29] We don't know why, but the body is immediately placed in a casket. Symbolically, a person is buried wearing his suit and tie (if he worked in one of the professions), with a new haircut, everything prepared as if he is alive. If he's a peasant, he is buried in his new *galabiyya* or robe,[30] that he usually wears on special occasions. But before the burial the body must be washed. In certain cultures the family takes care of the washing but in the Middle East, the family cannot even touch the body. So a volunteer or the undertaker washes the body before dressing him in a beautiful way.

The Coptic or Christian cemetery is really amazing.[31] It is like entering a village. People are never buried underground. Homes, sometimes very strange, and no doubt inspired by the tombs of the pharaohs are built. After six thousand years of history with some adjustments, Egyptian Christian cemeteries have now developed into communities of homes. My family has a home in a town where it lives, with a key and a door and locks. The house even has a kitchen, living rooms, and bedrooms. On certain feast occasions, the family of the deceased get the key from the oldest or the most respected man in the family, go to that house, open the door, and rest there for several days or a week. It's like vacationing in Las Vegas! Underneath the house is the basement where the caskets are lined up. Everybody knows this is the casket of so-and-so and so-and-so. When the family is endowed with a brilliant or famous man, there are sometimes special inscriptions. These family reunions in the cemetery house are often festive occasions, not gloomy funeral reminders. Family members console each other and the minister or priest offers a prayer and the family gives the priest a little money. When the family visits the house, they prepare *rahmah*. *Rahmah* is a form of charity. They make a big loaf of bread, and give it to poor people — who know that this is the day the Christians go to their tombs, and ask for it as charity. You will find many baskets full of bread. This also has symbolic meaning — for comfort of the soul of the deceased, wherever he may be. This custom is deeply embedded among the Christians, whether educated or rural people.

The Christians of the Middle East are a minority group. The predominant religion is Islam. In accordance with Muslim concepts of death and dying, loud screams and lamentations are performed only by women.[32] The women lock the room where the body is kept, stay in the living room, and begin to wail so that everybody in the neighborhood will know that somebody in this house died and a funeral is pending. The women hit their cheeks very hard until others stare, because it is believed that a woman who does not hit her cheeks hard and scream loudly doesn't love the dead person or lacks interest in him. Christians do the same.[33]

Another distinctive aspect of Muslim funeral practice involves a group of women called *naddābāt* or in the singular, *naddābah,* who come to the funeral house. Immediately after death a family member contacts one of these women. The woman brings a group with their drums, and they begin to eulogize the beautiful characteristics of the deceased. These women are very fiery and emotional. If they slow down, they are urged by relatives of the dead to pick up the tempo. Then they do all they can to raise their emotions. They cry out without interruption with no food, no drink all day until the body is prepared and washed and taken from the house to the burial place.

For Christians, we know where the dead are going. The dead have a home, or a semi-home at least. For Muslims, burial is very simple, the same from Nasser to Sadat to the man in the street. After the body is washed, it is wrapped in a white sheet. Instead of a casket, a flat board platform is used, held up by four assigned pallbearers and four volunteers. They rotate their positions from the home to the burial place. There are no automobiles with headlights on and no police officers to accompany the march as is done in the United States. But such a procession lets everyone know that a funeral is taking place. The people march until they reach the burial place on the outskirts of the city. Then they dig a simple hole large enough to accommodate the person. The deceased is taken from the board and placed in the hole. Dirt is thrown over him and burial is complete.

When I first came to Utah and attended the funeral I discussed earlier, I asked myself, "What do these people do?" The body of the dead is uncovered, the casket is half open, the person is embalmed and powdered to look natural. This struck me as the opposite of Muslim and Christian culture of Egypt or the Middle East. In the United States the deceased is kept for three or four days, sometimes a week, in a refrigerator in the mortuary until the funeral date is set, then people view the body.

To us the whole idea is entirely different. Who is a dying man? What does dying mean to Muslims? In the Muslim Qur'ān Muhammed said: "If you are a good man, God will be very pleased to meet you and you will be also very pleased to meet God." That means you go right away in a sputnik, you go directly to God and He will shake hands with you if you are a good man. If you are not a good man on earth, you will go to hell. Heaven and hell are there for good and bad people. In the Qur'ān, all Muslims are commanded to do well, to perform their Islamic duties, prayers, fasting, and all else.

Another feature of Middle Eastern funerals is that they do not end when the person is buried. Female relatives of the deceased return home where other women come to deliver their condolences. In the yard of the home a huge tent has been constructed, made of fancy cloth and decorated. As many as five hundred to six hundred chairs have been set out to handle the crowds. There is a special seat, the hands and arms of which are made of gold, placed there for the convenience of the *faqīh* who recites the Qur'ān. Whether you are poor or rich, this is one of the necessities of a bona fide Muslim funeral. After sunset, all the clan stand outside the tent on chairs, there receiving the condolences of others. When the *faqīh* pauses in his recitations, one group moves on and as he resumes, another group comes in. Coffee is offered, and it's a must to partake. I don't know how they do it now, when a pound of coffee costs five dollars, but tradition requires that the family, whether poor or rich must serve black coffee — very thick and very fine. There is a well-dressed waiter, hired of course, who circulates with a tray of coffee for the guests. You cannot say, "Thank you, I don't drink coffee.'' You have to drink it. If you don't drink it, it's a serious insult to the deceased.

This tent stays up for three days and then is dismantled. But the mourning period continues for forty days. The family of the deceased are in mourning, crying all this time. They do not eat until someone else comes in and pressures them to eat. They eat a little bite here and little bite there. Food is crucial. They never eat dessert or any sweets during these forty days and don't even put sugar in their coffee or tea.

On the fortieth day, regardless of whether you are Muslim or Christian, the ritual begins again. Professional female mourners are called in and the men receive their friends once more.

During these funeral rites men wear black ties. If you ever go to the Middle East and see a man wearing a black tie, that means he is in mourning. He may wear it for years, depending how dear or how close the dead person was to him. Women wear black dresses; everything is black. Some people in rural areas get black mascara and put it on their faces, forehead, and hands so that everyone will immediately see that they are in mourning. Black faces, black dresses, and black coffee are signs of mourning in Egypt. Some people even paint their windows black to show their distress and to express sorrow for the departure of a beloved relative or friend.

Another interesting custom in the Middle East is that radios cannot be played in homes surrounding the deceased's home. It's a tradition and to do so is very insulting. If I play a radio, the relatives of the deceased will hear the music and send a man to my house and tell me to turn off my radio. They have television in Egypt now and I don't know how the young people manage to miss the ''Six Million Dollar Man'' and the ''Bionic Woman.'' These customs and habits are always followed during times of mourning, whether you are poor or rich, whether you live in a village or in a city.

There is another interesting sign of death and dying in the Middle East. When the women scream and slap their faces, you will probably hear one word — *yāgamili* — ''Oh, my camel.'' The woman who cries this is the wife of the dead man. *Gamali* means ''my camel.'' She is saying, ''Oh, my camel.'' Of course he was not a camel, but it shows the great loss that has occurred. A camel symbolizes wealth among the villagers and when a camel dies naturally or disappears, it's a great loss. How about a man? He's the provider of the family. He does everything for the family. He's the man of the family. Therefore, he's the camel of the family, symbolic of the endurance of the camel, capable of crossing many miles in desert without even a sip of water.

There is segregation in Egyptian funeral rites. Women go into the house. They are not to go outside. Men only go outside. Even in rural areas, only certain women can go with the procession. If they are very close to the deceased, they can go to the tomb and attend the burial rituals. But most women stay home and wait for the funeral party to return.

Christians visit the tomb only on occasions like Christmas and Easter. They spend Christmas and Easter in the tomb sitting in the home. They sleep there three or four nights with the buried people underneath.

The Muslims go to the tomb every Thursday. They must go on that day, carrying with them palm branches and palm leaves. Each person walks in the street carrying a palm leaf. This is related to the concept of *raḥmah,* "mercy," or "charity." A green palm leaf is a symbol of mercy. It is an expression in Egypt similar to the American idea of visiting the dead with flowers.

I have touched upon the attitudes and customs of various Middle Eastern cultures toward the inevitable mystery of death. I trust, in this presentation, that you have received some valuable insights into death and dying as it relates to Egypt, Islam, and the Coptic faith. Hopefully this will serve to give you a better understanding of ways in which the traditions of the Middle East differ from those practiced in the United States, particularly among the Mormon people.

NOTES

1. *Hughes' Dictionary of Islam* (London, 1885), pp. 79-81.

2. Muslims wear *ihram* or simple white robes when participating in the pilgrimage to Mecca. The idea of paradisiacal clothing is also known among members of the Mormon faith.

3. Italics added by the author. Again, such a belief resembles the Muslim beliefs, i.e., white is the symbol of purity and blackness is the symbol of sin.

4. Reminiscent of the words of Jesus in the New Testament, Mark 10:25.

5. The origin of the American word "sherbet"?

6. A water well which is considered holy water by all Muslims who perform the annual pilgrimage to Mecca.

7. In Arabic, *Bukhūr*.

8. As in the case of Eastern Christians and Jews.

9. A common habit among Middle Eastern people.

10. This has reference to washing the body of the deceased.

11. A Muslim ritual of purification performed before entering the Mosque.

12. A white sheet of cloth to cover the lower parts of the body.

13. This means a "shirt."

14. *Lifāfah* is an Arabic word derived from the root *laffa,* "to wrap up."

15. A poor person.

16. *Hughes' Dictionary of Islam,* pp. 79-81. Nowadays in the Middle East the family of the deceased goes to the grave carrying a palm tree leaf to put on the grave instead of flowers. Here we can see cultural interplay. Flowers in the Middle East are still considered a sign of joy, but a palm leaf is not so joyful.

17. Arthur Jefrey, *A Reader on Islam* (Houston, 1962), p. 197.

18. The two words *bashīr* and *nadhīr,* used in this Tradition, are said to have become technical terms in pre-Islamic Mecca, the *bashīr* being the announcer of good news of a caravan's safe arrival, and the *nadhir* being the announcer of the bad news that a caravan had been lost. (Compare bashīr with the term *bishārah* which is applicable only to the New Testament.)

19. *Marārat al-mawt,* "the distress of death," has reference to one of the many expressions used for death-pains or the agony of death.

20. I.e., they would be so terrified that they would always be thin and lean.

21. *Sakrat al-mawt* is another of the many expressions for the agony of death, or the last moments before death.

22. Those who are loyal or sincere.

23. Plural of *waliyy,* which means a friend, a beloved, a tutor, a patron, a guardian, and in some contexts, a saint. It may be noted that the Guardian Angels are beings identified here with the Recording Angels, though generally they are kept distinct.

24. An Arab word which means "the supporters of the Prophet."

25. Sūra LXXXIII, 18-21. It is said to be a place in the uppermost heaven where the record of the righteous is kept.

26. These are *Munkar* and *Nakīr,* the blue-eyed questioners of the dead.

27. Sūra LXXXIII, 7-9; in Arabic it means "prison".

28. This is elaborated in Frazer's classic work, *The Golden Bough*.

29. Unless death occurred at night. In this case, the funeral rites are administered next day as early as possible.

30. Peasants, especially in Egypt, instead of a suit wear a garment which is called *galabiyya* or *quftān*.

31. There is no serious research on the burial customs of the Copts in Egypt. However, the writer is planning to conduct such research in the near future.

32. The Christians and Jews follow the same procedures, with some variations from one denomination to another.

33. Among the upper classes, this pattern is not followed in most cases.

3

Distinctions in the Mormon Approach to Death and Dying

Truman G. Madsen

This symposium corroborates a recent essay on ''Dying with Dignity'' that reports a ''crescendo of concern'' about dying and death.[1] The concern shows up in books, journals, conferences, television programs, societies. Yet, at the same time, it is observed that, whereas the facts of life were hidden from youth in a former generation, the facts of death seem to be a conversational taboo today. How does one reconcile this deliberate avalanche of discussion and studied silence?

A score of writers would argue that this paradox arises because we try to make death a ''thing'' outside of us — vague, anonymous, removed — an escape from the gnawing awareness in all of us that we must die. Our preoccupation can be deliberately ignored as it is in silence, or it can emerge in all kinds of brave verbal objectifications.

If Latter-day Saints are unimpressed by these trends, it is not due, I suspect, to isolation or insulation from the real world. It is because there are root assurances that go deep and overbeliefs that go high; these preside over and temper all of our attitudes. In this paper I wish to address ten such roots of Mormon assurance which are powerful in their patterning effect.

My title uses the word "distinctions." The first question is, are the distinctions distinctive? In three ways they are not: First, if one looks deeply into historic religions, he can find precedent, parallel, and in some cases identity in the teachings of this dispensation and those of former ones. Second, the response to death, both in individuals and in institutions, undergoes change. Our great-grandfathers may have had significantly different attitudes about death, though they belonged to the same or a most similar religious movement. Third, the doctrinal or teaching core of the Church on this theme is overlaid with multiple ever-expanding cultures. Many of the variable customs and traditions of other cultures may or may not be harmonious with this gospel outlook but continue to have residual influence on the convert.

Plurality

One striking insight in the Mormon scriptures on death is that there are many kinds. The word itself is often used in the plural, "deaths," in exact juxtaposition to the word "lives." The point here is not simply that there are many ways of reaching the final event of mortality, it is, rather, that while we are more or less alive here, there are many possible dyings. Without being too precise, one finds in the scriptures at least four characterizations of death: (1.) Death is absence from the presence of God. (2.) Death is the wages of sin — the loss of life intensity. It is, for example, darkness of mind, hardness of heart and numbness of conscience. These are the deaths in the self which may precede death of the body. The deceased is diseased spiritually. (3.) Death is the separation of the spirit from the body. (4.) Death is the discontinuation of life powers. This is the opposite of what Section 132 calls "the fullness and continuation of the seeds" — a delimitation on creative and pro-creative power.

The role of Christ is to overcome all of these deaths in us, both as prevention and redemption. To gain victory over every form of death is the essence of life. Preoccupation with the third kind, the event, is a sign of confusion: soul-sickness. "Salvation consists in overcoming all one's enemies. The last enemy is death.''

Death and God

In the world's major religions, the question of God and the question of immortality are often separate: one may affirm the one and deny the other. Belief in immortality has never been strong among the Jews, for example, yet belief in God has been vigorous. Among philosophers, Charles Hartshorne is not alone in affirming a life-giving and fully perfected God who not only permits but requires that man disappear forever. On the other hand, there are those who affirm immortality and deny God. Scientists today, by no means mad scientists, seriously reach for the dream of Ponce de Leon. Some say we will be capable of immortality before the turn of the century. We may even opt to die with tentative rights for a rerun on the demand of our survivors — blanking out for periods and blinking in for other periods. Then the folk witticism would be practical: ''If the rich could hire others to die, a poor man could make a living.''[2]

Mormonism, whatever the triumphs of the scientists, equates God, immortality, and resurrection. Life in its highest mode requires all three. There is a difference between surviving forever and living forever. One who achieves eternal life must have become like the eternal who has mastered life — he must be perfect.

What Death Does to Life

In contemporary discussion, opposite attitudes arise as one faces imminent death. For Martin Heidegger, man at his best is committed to whatever he does as *Sein-zum-Tode* — being unto death. For him, the consciousness of death at this level is intertwined with the sense of the passing of time, projects, and guilt. On different grounds, Jean-Paul Sartre and Camus affirm the essence of ''living on the underground,'' the constant threat of death as somehow leading to the existential virtue of authenticity. One is most alive when he is closest to death. On other grounds,

Viktor Frankl recalls his prison camp experience as his clearest and closest understanding of love.

For Joseph Smith, death is indeed the outside limit and sometimes the cost of a Christ-like mission. There may be slow martyrdom, as when one "wastes and wears out his life" in bringing to light hidden things of darkness. "Be faithful, even if you should be slain," he was told early. Or death may fulfill, atone, redeem. "Do not be alarmed, brethren, for they can only do what they did to the ancient saints. They can only kill the body." To the degree that this statement of Joseph Smith in the menace of a mob comforted his brethren, they had caught the vision. But notice that for Joseph Smith death was not a mere incident because the body is cheap or worthless. Rather, it was because the body is finally indestructible. The quality of man's resurrection depends upon his response to the way of Christ. To preserve the mortal body by betrayal of Christ is a death worse than death.

The Body As Enemy

In many religions, ancient and modern, the body is viewed as an impediment to the spiritual life, a prison or as Plato put it, "an outlandish slough," a Gnostic prison. Among Buddhists the body or *skhanda* is finally recognized as inferior and even as unreal. So likewise in Christian Science. In the religions of escape in the Far East, persistence of life in the body is viewed as the extension of *karma,* a kind of punishment. And where the objective is not utter annihilation, the body is to be deprived and mortified but with the high aim to achieve the extinction of desire. In monastic Catholic traditions and pious Protestant ones, there is a similar effort, often ascribed to Paul, that takes initiative in asceticism. Gandhi expressed two world traditions, occidental and oriental, in saying he wished he had never experienced fleshly impulses.

Contrary to these views, much Greek philosophical theology, and the flesh-disparagements of Augustine and Calvin, Mormonism teaches:

1. That "we came into the world to receive a body and present it pure before God in the Celestial Kingdom." That op-

pression in our pre-embodied condition arose because we lacked a body.

"All beings who have bodies have power over those who have not."[3]

As Joseph Smith put it, "The express purpose of God in giving it (the spirit) a tabernacle was to arm it against the power of darkness."[4] And elsewhere he taught that unembodied intelligences did not have power to defend themselves against those that had a tabernacle. It is a privilege to be in the body, even a crippled, handicapped, diseased body.

2. That the purpose of life is not to transcend the flesh but to transform it. "The great principle of happiness consists in having a body."

3. That a fulness of joy is impossible without the inseparable connection of spirit and body. "When separated man cannot receive a fulness of joy."[5]

4. That we should improve the time of this mortal probation because, "A man can do as much in this life in one year as he can do in ten years in the spirit world without the body."[6]

5. That the strong will to endure life, even in the midst of pain, has been divinely planted in us in order that we might cling to life and thus accomplish the designs of our Creator. So said Joseph Smith to Wilford Woodruff.[7]

6. That there is some truth in the comment, "The good die young," because, as Joseph speculated, they are "too pure, too lovely to live upon the earth."[8] Yet in the long view Joseph Smith taught, "I do not like to see a little child pass away, for it has not filled the measure of its creation and gained the victory over death."[9] Children, of course, are innocent, but they are not experienced. They will yet have opportunities of reckoning in the flesh with experience and contrast, if only in the post-millennial struggle. They are assured salvation in the celestial kingdom, but only when they have fulfilled the conditions will they enjoy the highest exaltation.

7. That desire, fulfillment of desires and increased refinement of desire, are eternal processes.

8. That death as a separation process is an enemy. The spirit may properly crave death (due to the decline of age, disease, and

the imprisoning effects of sin), but we will look upon the absence of our spirits from our bodies as "a bondage."[10]

Selective vs. Universal Immortality

Many world religions hold that death is universal but that immortality is extremely selective, reserved for the elite, the few, the 144,000, the fit, the enlightened ones, or whatever. (Some religions deny that some men even have souls and have certainly excluded animals and the lower forms of life.) Joseph Smith said, "All are born to die. And all men must rise." "All must enter eternity." Man is not an endangered species.

As for other forms of life, Joseph Smith taught, "Every living thing that knows enough to run when you point your finger at it will be resurrected."[11] That means not just beasts, fish, and birds; it means ants, beetles (of whom there are nine thousand known species), and mosquitoes. Joseph taught that John's apocalypse speaks of beasts in heaven, not only in rich symbolisms, but in literal description: there are beasts in heaven. He taught, according to Benjamin F. Johnson, that all the animal kingdoms resurrected "would remain in the dominion and therefore the stewardship of those who, with creative power, reach out for dominion through the power of endless lives." He expected, he said, to meet his black horse Joe Duncan and his faithful dog Major.

The Earth Glorified

If life is precious in animal form, it is also precious in plant and mineral. God commends all life. The earth itself is organic, somehow alive. In the sense of separation of spirit and body, it will eventually die. It will die, moreover, innocently. Unlike rebellious man, the earth flawlessly fills the measure of its creation — obeys the law of its organizer. Too often man has not replenished but exploited, not sanctified but polluted, not redeemed but corrupted the earth. The earth has been baptized by immersion, it will likewise be baptized in the Spirit by fire, be renewed to its paradisaical state, and glorified to a beauty beyond description.[12] It will then return to its position in the cosmos from which it was removed after the fall of man. It will be "rolled back into the presence of God." Not the least but the most righteous will inherit it.

Thus the history of Mother Earth recapitulates the history of sanctified mankind. And it is a type, a foreshadowing, of more and more worlds that are more and more alive, abundant, and abounding. Christ and the resurrected Saints will reign upon it during the one thousand years, but not permanently, for they will thereafter "come and go, visiting and governing the earth." So Edward L. Stevenson heard Joseph say.[13] The kinship of life and life will be complete. There will be no need for C. S. Lewis's imaginative proposal for rewarding insects. "A heaven for mosquitoes could be combined with a hell for man." Heaven will be the same for both.

Is All of Real Man Immortal?

It is not uncommon in world religions to hold that only one aspect or fragment or faculty or mode of man will live on. For Plato, this is the immaterial soul. For Aristotle, it is *nous* or reason. For the Buddhists, it is the ultimate nature of the enlightened *bodhi* in a distinctionless nirvana. For the Christian Scientist, it is pure mind.

Joseph Smith taught that all of real man is immortal: mind, spirit and body. Therefore the analogy of similarity between the conditions we know here and the conditions hereafter is thoroughgoing. But there are crucial differences. The most vital change between the present corruptible body and the incorrupt resurrection is that the glorified body will have within it not blood, but a spirit fluid. "Flesh and blood cannot go there, but flesh and bones quickened by the Spirit of God can."[14] For Joseph Smith, there are everlasting spirals of unfolding involvement, self-sacrificing love — "all heights and all depths." Eternal lives will include the contemplative, the active, and the creative modes, greatly intensified into the magnificence of celestial joy.

Importance of Probation

The notion of transmigration of souls or of successive mortal rebirths or of switching species was labeled by Joseph Smith as "a doctrine of the devil."[15]

The doctrine is wrongheaded for three reasons: First, "All men must die and all must rise" (in their own bodies). This is the law. It cancels out all variations of doctrines of body switching or soul sleeping, as also of annihilation. Second, there is no cross-over of kinds. Men do not become cockroaches, nor vice versa; sacred cows do not become gods. Our body, the body we have now in its essential elements is ours forever. The decision to accept embodiment was voluntary. Now that it is made, it is irreversible. Your body is as permanently yours as you are permanently you. Even the sons of perdition will be resurrected.

Third, there is only one mortal probation, and it is crucial. There are stages before and stages after, and one may indeed move in the cyclic spiral, but not in repetition and not in a circle. The seriousness, the risk, and the glories of mortal life are undercut the moment one supposes he will have a million or more subsequent probations of the same sort. It is a spurious comfort to be told, as was the weeping wife at the cremation of her husband in India, "Do not weep, he has been through this a million times before." Physically and metaphysically that is impossible.

This also means that ontological suicide — the craving for annihilation — is a will-o'-the-wisp. The positive gospel message is: we must learn to live with ourselves.

The Quantity-Quality Controversy

Many who believe immortality is an illusion, religious humanists for example, insist that both suicide and euthanasia are a human right. If there is, as Freud taught, a death wish, some claim that it is more than a desire to end this predicament and indeed all predicaments; it is a desire for "the catastrophe which ends all catastrophe." Will Durrant says in effect, that after writing thirty-five volumes, "eternal sleep will be welcome." Other humanists argue that there is something hypocritical, spurious, or projective about the religious notion that one should live for the next life instead of for this one. Secular critics such as Marx and Feurbrach plead for living exclusively in the here and now.

No religion has been as effective as Mormonism in uniting the traditional split between the here and now and the then and there. The spirit and body are inseparably connected; so in the temples are heaven and earth; so are joy and sorrow; so are life and death. When Henry P. Van Dusen, President of Union Theological Seminary, and his wife committed suicide, some defended their right. But others, feeling this was a betrayal of both life and death, said sadly, ''We do not read in the New Testament that man has a right, on his own, to decide when to lay down his cross.'' Mormons share that conviction.

The Family As an Individual

Much of Judeo-Christian theology doubts or denies individual immortality: so do scientific materialists. The self is swallowed up in some cosmic reservoir, as absolute as in Bertrand Russell's ''vast, total death of the solar system.'' Some have nevertheless offered the comfort of ''social immortality.'' This means that one is replicated in his posterity, or at least in the memory of friends.

We have observed that Joseph Smith teaches individual identity in perpetuity in both directions. In this sense, our individual immortality is in no way contingent on that of others. On the other hand, the highest immortality is a family affair. In that sense we are either exalted together or not at all. Thus, others are crucial to the quality and intensity of our own eternal lives. Husband and wife become ''one'' in their children. But parents are themselves linked to an unbroken chain of forebears. This is a clarification of the great Israelite insight that all Israel and ultimately all mankind stand accountable and privileged before God as one individual. We do not overcome what Joseph Smith called the ''last enemy,'' which is death, until we perceive that ''they without us and we without them cannot be made perfect,'' hence the indispensability of sealing in its highest, deepest sense. This is the core of truth in the oriental notion that our ancestors may both plague us and bless us. The positive truth is that to some extent they may redeem us as we them, and that our highest transformation is interwined with theirs.

We may miss this crucial point when we say that the resurrection is unconditional, but that redemption from sin is conditional upon Christ. In fact, the thatness of *a* resurrection is inevitable. But the when, the how, the where, and the by whom; the withness of our and their resurrection, is contingent not only on Brother Christ but on all brothers elder and younger, the whole family of Christ. In no world religion is this theme more central, more conscious, and more extensively carried out in action.

Death and Fatalism

Is the time of death preset? There are determinist religions that say yes. Among the Greek Stoics, submission to the necessity of death, including its timing, was the essence of wisdom. Among the Romans, the Greek idea of *moira* or destiny became the trump card of human courage. Shakespeare has Julius Caesar say he has no fear because "Death, a necessary end, will come when it will come." In the Orient there is *Kismet* (fate), a denial at times of any chance or voluntary factors in the life and death process. In America we are told that one of every five citizens today believes somehow in astrology, and among the things the stars are believed to control is the time of death. The man who asked the spiritualist where he was going to die exclaimed, "I'll never go there!" But the point of Greek tragedy, as of modern determinism, is that we have no choice.

Mormonism is not with the fatalists. It is true that modern revelation speaks of being "appointed unto death."[16] And the Prophet Joseph Smith was promised in Liberty Jail, "Thy days are known, and thy years shall not be numbered less."[17] (The inference is also, shall not be numbered more.) The assurance is not uncommon among Latter-day Saints that whereas the wicked may shorten their lives, the righteous are taken only when "their time" has come.

In fact, these promises are all conditional. Life may be prolonged by the united efforts of the faithful. Joseph's exact promise was that *if* he hearkened unto the voice of the Spirit, he had *about* five years to live. The "if" clause, as well as the inexactness of the time, left room for his initiative. Promises to the faithful of protection, of fulfillment of missions, of safety arise not as an independent, relentless, grinding fate, but as the result of a free-willed covenant relationship in which both the will of man and the will of God collude. Only so long as one is true and faithful does one have promise; otherwise he has none.

Mourning Customs

The variations on meeting the dazing shock of death are almost infinite. Among the Jews, the first response is a *shiva,* a seven-day period of mourning. One remains at home, seated in the midst of sympathizing friends. Then comes *shloshim;* one avoids places of entertainment and follows ritual prayers. For parents this is followed by a full year of mourning. Comparable practices exist in other world religions.

Among the Mormons there is no valorizing or ceremonializing of mourning, though there is a characteristic funeral. Modern revelation admonishes, "Thou shalt weep for the loss of thy loved ones, especially those who have not hope of a glorious resurrection." The promise "Those that die in me shall not taste [the bitterness of] death, for it shall be sweet unto them"[18] extends often to those bereaved. When death comes at a ripe climax of a life well lived, there is a noticeable absence of agony, a fervent sense of culmination, and even, at times, rejoicing.

Having worked four years in a cemetery witnessing funerals, graveside rituals, and patterns of almost every nationality, tradition, and emotional tone, I can report this: the closest analogy to a Mormon funeral at graveside is a missionary farewell. Here is a group of loved ones, not hard-faced and stoical, not blank and numb, but sensitized. There is apparent grief, but not despair. There is warmth and promise. This may be caught up in the words of Wilford Woodruff and then in a list of impressions otherwise unaccountable. First, President Woodruff:

> . . . I wish my body washed clean and clothed in clean white linen, according to the order of the Holy Priesthood, and put

> into a plain, decent coffin, made of native wood, with plenty of room. *I do not wish any black made use of about my coffin, or about the vehicle that conveys my body to the grave.* I do not wish my family or friends *to wear any badge of mourning for me* at my funeral or afterwards, for, if I am true and faithful unto death, there will be no necessity for anyone to mourn for me. . . . Their speech will be to the living. *If the laws and customs of the spirit world will permit, I should wish to attend my funeral but I shall be governed by the counsel I receive in the spirit world.*[19]

Now the list of impressions:

— The ancient mother who cheerfully sews her own white burial clothes.

— The widely known speaker who tapes his own funeral sermon and sparkles it with his verve for life.

— A gathering, as death hovers close, to appoint a celestial mailman. Messages to be delivered to loved ones on the other side. "Give my love to Mother," or "Tell Aunt Martha we're doing fine." Here is absent the curious etiquette that forbids that even a husband and wife use the word "death" when one knows clearly that one is on his deathbed.

— Humor that is neither grizzly nor forced, that enables a man emerging from a stroke to wink his one good eye and say to the family anxiously surrounding his bed, "I fooled you!"

— Addressing the deceased at the funeral or graveside as if she or he is present.

— The smile that so often attends the faithful, as if the last mortal facial set was in recognition of a beckoning loved one.

— The sense of mission in the military. Facing death is the price of Christ's way.

— The music which resembles a hymnal rhapsody rather than the darkening dirge. "And may there be no sadness of farewell, when I embark." (Tennyson.)

— The jibe of a J. Golden Kimball: "I can't wait to die to see if all this stuff we've been teaching is true," combined with the sober testimony, "When I meet my Father, I know he will understand me, and that is more than you have been able to do."

— Prompt and some would say sudden remarriage. Joseph Smith followed the early custom of thinking marriage within three months was unkind to the memory of the dead but reversed himself when he counseled his brother Hyrum to marry "without delay."[20]

Sacred Ground

Is the burial place sacred? In many religions, yes. Trespass onto Indian burial grounds is met with capital punishment. The excessive luxuriance of the pharaohs in mummification, rich artifacts, and pyramidal protection is an attempt to foil the sacrilege of gravediggers. In many churches, Catholic and Protestant, over the centuries the right to be buried in or near the churchyard has functioned as a spiritual badge or as posthumous excommunication.

Mormonism both affirms and denies these traditions. On the one hand, Joseph Smith praised and reembodied the desires of the ancient Joseph to have his bones brought back to the family tomb in Shechem. Before he undertook the perilous Zion's Camp march, he charged Brigham Young to bring his body back to Kirtland. "I command you to do it in the name of Israel's God," and learning that missionary Lorenzo Barnes was being buried on foreign soil, he developed that theme. Late in 1844 he told his trusted brethren Alpheus Cutler and Reynolds Cahoon that he wanted to be buried by his father in a Nauvoo tomb, unless his enemies preempted his body as they had threatened. Likewise, he made the same request of Emma. John Taylor recalls his reason for this; it was future-oriented.

> I heard Joseph Smith say at the time he was making a tomb at Nauvoo that he expected when the time came, when the grave would be rent asunder, that he would arise and embrace his father and mother, and shake hands with his friends. It was his written request that when he died, some kind friends would see he was buried near his bosom friends, so that when he and they arose in the morning of the First Resurrection, he could embrace them, saying, "My father! My mother!"[21]

Conclusion

One reading of much that I have said is that, for the Mormons, death is an illusion. There could not be a more fatal mistake. The mortal predicament is not simply that we have a deadline beyond which the body will temporarily dissolve; it is that while still in the body, we may so imbibe the poisons of sin that we suffer, in more or less degree, the permanent blows of death. One key for understanding all of the ordinances of the gospel, beginning with the rebirths of baptism and culminating in the sealings of the temple, is that all are instruments of overcoming both death *of* the body and death *in* the body.

In Mormon theology the adversary is the arch-destroyer; his diabolical objective is to clip the wings of life. To the degree that he diminishes life he is winning, as we are losing. It is a tragic confusion to suppose that his winning is temporary. He has already won one-third of the hosts of heaven against embodiment, plunging them into a lasting death. He is in a life-and-death struggle with all of mankind on an even broader scale. We may rejoice that "all will be saved except the sons of perdition." But to be saved, even to be exalted in a delimited condition is to be partially damned.

Jacob prays: "May God raise you from death by the power of the resurrection, and also from everlasting death by the power of the atonement, that ye may be received into the eternal kingdom of God, that ye may praise him through grace divine. Amen."[22]

NOTES

1. Foreword to "The Favor of the Gods," annual oration of the Society for Health and Human Values, by Ronald Berman, San Francisco, California, November 11, 1976.

2. *Sholem Aleichem.*

3. From William Clayton's book, p. 8, MS 188, Brigham Young University Special Collections, Provo, Utah.

4. See Minute Book of William P. McIntyre, January 8, 1840-April 20, 1845, MSC 1014, Historical Department of The Church of Jesus Christ of Latter-day Saints, Salt Lake City, Utah.

5. D&C 93:33.

6. See Oliver B. Huntington in *They Knew the Prophet* (Salt Lake City: Bookcraft, 1974), p. 61.

7. See Diary of Charles L. Walker, August, 1877, St. George, p. 576, BYU Special Collections.

8. Joseph Smith, *Teachings of the Prophet Joseph Smith,* comp. Joseph Fielding Smith (Salt Lake City: Deseret Book Co., 1938), p. 196.

9. See *Early History of Provo,* 1849-1872; Utah Stake Bishop Meetings, July 17, 1868.

10. See D&C 45:17.

11. YWJ, V:490.

12. D&C 84:25-26.

13. Edward L. Stevenson, *Life of Edward Stevenson,* BYU Special Collections, p. 104.

14. Joseph Smith, *Teachings of the Prophet Joseph Smith,* p. 326.

15. Joseph Smith, *Teachings of the Prophet Joseph Smith,* pp. 104-105.

16. D&C 42:48.

17. D&C 122:9.

18. D&C 42:46.

19. Mathias Cowley, "Wilford Woodruff," *Deseret News,* 1909, p. 622.

20. Joseph Smith, *Teachings of the Prophet Joseph Smith,* p. 120.

21. John Taylor, *Gospel Kingdom* (Salt Lake City: Bookcraft, 1943), p. 23.

22. 2 Nephi 10:25.

Deity and the Divine

A Comparative Study of Ascension Motifs in World Religions

4

Edward T. Jones

Diogenes of Sinope once listened to a philosopher speaking about celestial matters. Diogenes approached and asked him: "When did you come back from heaven?"[1] Those who sit and listen to speakers discourse about the heavens have a right, perhaps an obligation, to determine the authority by which the speaker so discourses. Is he speaking from personal experience or merely the hearsay of another? Joseph Smith declared that men speak of heaven and hell and have seen neither; he further taught that if a man could gaze into heaven for the space of five minutes, he would learn more than had ever been written on the subject.[2]

The records of the religious world and even the non-religious world are filled with accounts of individuals who did in fact visit heaven and return, or at least claimed to have visited the other worlds. These accounts are found throughout the world, in ancient written documents and in modern verbal traditions handed down within the different cultures. The purpose of this paper will be to investigate and discuss several such experiences, comparing them with each other and seeking to draw out of these accounts the common elements. Some effort will also be made to interpret the data as well as is possible on the basis of the common features.

The technical term for the experience of visiting heaven is ascension. As Mircea Eliade has indicated, it is "one of the oldest religious means of personally communicating with the Gods."[3] The most obvious and well-known example is that of Jesus ascending to heaven following his death and resurrection. This is a special case, however, and lies outside the realm of this paper. A better example would be his descent into hell to visit and release those souls who resided there. Technically this is known as a *descensus* rather than an ascension, but basically the only distinction is the direction traveled and the condition of those visited or seen (heaven contains God and other divine beings and perhaps the righteous dead, whereas hell contains devils and other evil beings, as well as the souls of the wicked). Because many of those who visited heaven also visited hell, both experiences will come under the domain of this paper.

Another example well known in the Western world is that of Paul, who intimated that he had visited the third heaven and paradise and seen there things which were not possible to be communicated to men (2 Corinthians 12:1-4). This experience was further developed by later Christian writers who used his name and will be discussed below. Other better-known examples would be those of Enoch and Elijah, who were translated into heaven without experiencing death. Again, however, these two are types somewhat different from those to be the main study of this paper. The experiences of all these men are duplicated throughout the world, sometimes with great similarities, other times with lesser areas of agreement.

Jean Danielou defines ascension as:

> the raising up of a person above the heavens . . . and is susceptible of various interpretations, the most ancient being that which was used to describe the elevation of a visionary . . . so that he is able to contemplate the heavenly world normally hidden from his eyes.[4]

An old Hebrew midrash states that God gives man a preliminary disclosure of the secrets of the other world in order to allow the righteous to die in peace.[5]

The ascension motif can be divided into three rather distinct groupings. The first is that of the initial calling of the individual to a new consecrated level of behavior, i.e., the prophet or shaman. The second is that of the "out of the body experience" which is so much written about today. This latter has occurred often and is of the type of Paul's experience. The third type is the ritual ascension which kings often underwent at New Year rituals, but which also often involved other individuals. The ritual ascension is obviously not a real ascension into heaven, but may be based upon some such real experience by an ancestor or other cultural hero.[6] The two types of ascension, the "real" or "spiritual" ("Whether in the body or out of the body I cannot tell" were the words Paul used), and the ritual would appear to be intimately related. There are many areas in which they overlap and deal with the same points. The ritual ascension will figure only slightly in this paper, mainly in the interpretation of the data. The ascension motifs (for now we can speak of several types) will be studied in the context of five major religious traditions: the Hebrew, Christian, Muslim, Hindu, and Buddhist.

The King James Version of Amos 3:7 reads: "Surely the Lord God will do nothing, but he revealeth his secret unto his servants the prophets." The word translated "secret" is Hebrew: *sodh*, which also means, and in many places of the Hebrew Bible is so translated, council. It refers to a council which works with God in the heavens. Consequently, another translation of this passage would be that God "revealeth his counsel unto the Prophets." In the book of Jeremiah (23:18, 21-22) there is a specific example of this:

> For who hath stood in the counsel of the Lord, and hath perceived and heard his word? who hath marked his word, and heard it? . . . I have not sent these [false] prophets, yet they ran: I have not spoken to them, yet they prophesied. But if they had stood in my counsel, and had caused my people to hear my words, then they should have turned them from their evil way, and from the evil of their doings.

The true prophet is here identified as the one who has stood in that heavenly council (*sodh*) and heard the words of God, which the prophet was then sent to declare to the people. The false prophets had not stood in that council.

Micah, however, had stood in that council and was a true prophet. He stated:

> I saw the Lord sitting on his throne, and all the host of heaven standing by him on his right hand and on his left. And the Lord said, Who shall persuade Ahab? . . . .one said on this manner, and another said on that manner. And there came forth a spirit, and stood before the Lord, and said, I will persuade him." (1 Kings 22:19-21)

H. Wheeler Robinson, in his study on "The Council of Yahweh," wrote that "the council of Yahweh was felt to be just as much a reality as Yahweh himself," and that the experience related about Micah in 1 Kings 22 "is offered quite seriously as a description of something which has actually taken place in heaven."[7]

More recently Patrick Miller has written that the

> conception of a divine assembly around the throne of Yahweh formed a basic element in the Israelite understanding of prophecy. The prophet was one who stood in the council of Yahweh. His task was the proclamation of the will and message of Yahweh as declared in the heavenly assembly.

Miller continued to say that "Jeremiah is very explicit about the fact that the true prophet has stood in the council of Yahweh."[8] Ezekiel and Isaiah also received their callings by ascending into heaven and standing in the presence of that assembly.[9]

In the Testament of the Twelve Patriarchs, there is an account of Levi being set apart as the head of the priestly clan. It is there recorded that Michael the archangel came and took Levi into heaven and presented him before the Lord. The Lord stretched forth his hand and blessed Levi that he and his sons after him would be holy to the Lord and would serve Him in the priestly office.[10]

Another example is that of the calling of Lehi in the Book of

Mormon. As recorded by his son Nephi, Lehi had a vision in which he saw the heavens opened and the throne of God, with God sitting upon it. A man was seen descending, who came to Lehi with a book which he bade him read. Lehi was then sent out as a prophet to cry repentance to the people of Jerusalem.[11]

As mentioned above, God often gave the righteous a foretaste of heaven by bringing them up for a look before they died. Virtually all the major personalities of the Hebrew Bible had such experiences, whether they were prophets or not: Adam, Seth, Enoch, Abraham, Isaac, Jacob, Levi, Moses, Elijah, Micah, Isaiah, Ezekiel, Jeremiah, and Baruch, his scribe.[12] The experiences of Abraham and Moses will be given here as representative of this group.

Following his battle with the kings and his meeting with Melchizedek, king of Salem, Abraham had a vision which is recorded in Genesis 15:

> The word of the Lord came unto Abram in a vision. . . . And he brought [Abraham] forth abroad, and said, Look now toward heaven, and tell the stars, if thou be able to number them. (verses 1-5)

The rabbis interpreted this as an ascension, that God "showed him the streets of heaven," and that God "lifted him up above the vault of heaven."[13] The Qur'ān (6.76) stated that God showed Abraham the kingdom of the heavens and the earth, that he might be of those "possessing certainty."

In the Apocalypse of Abraham (ca. A.D. 100), a Jewish work, Abraham is commanded to fast, which he does for a period of forty days (chapters ix, xii). He is then carried aloft by the angel (xv); in heaven he is given a vision of the premortal life wherein certain ones were foreordained to be of Abraham's lineage (xxii). He is also given a vision of that which will occur at the end of days, when ten plagues will affect mankind (xxx). Among those plagues are hunger, conflagration, earthquakes, and much snow.[14]

There is another text entitled the Testament of Abraham (ca. A.D. 30), which is quite distinct from the one above. This text, also Jewish in origin, tells of the angel Michael being sent by God to Abraham to bring him home at the end of his life. Abraham at first refuses to die, but then agrees when given the promise of any blessing he would ask. He asks that he might be allowed to see paradise while in the body, "so I can depart without sorrow." He is carried aloft once more, where he views the first gate of paradise at which Adam sits. There are in fact two gates shown him, one of them wide and the other narrow, through which the righteous, who are few in number, pass. Abraham is then given a vision of the world and sees the wickedness of those who are engaged in sin. He immediately requests that the earth open and swallow the guilty. He is then shown the punishment the guilty receive in hell. He is greatly sorrowed and ceases condemning those who sin. He then notices that there is one soul who is halted between the two doors. He is told that this man's merits and demerits are exactly equal to each other, but that he could be allowed into the narrow door for the righteous if Abraham would only offer a prayer for him. Abraham does and the man is saved in paradise. He then returns to earth, and upon his death angels take his body in "divinely woven linnen" and anoint it with oil.[15]

Several patriarchs between Abraham and Moses viewed heaven, but those accounts will not be examined here. Moses had three ascension experiences.[16] The first occurred at the burning bush when he was called to lead the people of Israel out of Egypt. Enoch was sent to carry him to heaven and guide him through the seven levels of heaven. His body was changed gradually as he progressed through each of them, more and more approximating that of those who reside in the highest. In the fourth heaven is the heavenly Temple, where angels enter and sing praises of God. In the seventh is God Himself. Moses also noticed an angel who was busy teaching souls in this "college on high."[17] He also read the Torah in the seventh heaven. Gabriel then showed Moses hell with its tortures, explaining each of the causes of the various tortures. He was then shown paradise, which contains the tree of life, beneath which flows a river. An angel sitting near the tree asked him why he was there, in response to which Moses stated: "To see the reward of the pious." He saw Abraham sitting on the biggest throne (other than the Lord's), with Isaac, Jacob, the prophets, saints, and the righteous souls sitting on others. He was told that the efforts of a pious son could gain a throne for an unrighteous father (Abraham's efforts in behalf of his idolatrous father Terah being the great example throughout Jewish history).[18] He was then given a vision of the future.

His second ascension experience took place on Mount Sinai. He then spent forty days in heaven, learning and receiving the Torah. Again he saw the seven heavens and the heavenly Temple, as well as the future.[19]

His final ascension came just prior to his death. As with Abraham, an angel was sent, but Moses refused to die until he was allowed to view heaven. He saw the Temple, the Messiah, his brother Aaron, his own throne prepared for him, as well as another vision of the future.[20] He stated at the end of his life:

> I ascended heaven and trod out a path there, and engaged in battle with the angels, and received the law of fire and sojourned under [God's] throne of fire, and took shelter under the pillar of fire, and spoke with God face to face; and I prevailed over the heavenly familia, and revealed unto the sons of man their secrets, and received the Law from the right hand of God, and taught it to Israel.[21]

The early Christian church accepted the legends which they received from the Jews regarding the earlier ascensions. Although many others received ascensions, only the experiences of Paul and Jesus will be discussed here.[22]

Paul in 2 Corinthians 12:1-4 describes an experience he had had some fourteen years previous to writing the letter (i.e., about A.D. 42). He states that he had seen the third heaven and paradise and had seen there things which he could not pass on to others. The Apocalypse of Paul (ca. A.D. 350-400) was written to give details of this visit to the other world. An angel carried Paul up to the third heaven where he saw the prophets and patriarchs of the Old Testament, along with thrones prepared for the righteous of the heathen nations. He saw the paradise of the Garden of Eden, and also hell, and the tortures meted out to the wicked. He saw a vision of those who wasted their time here on earth and were now paying for it in hell. He then saw Michael visit them and tell them to repent, that he was personally praying for them, and that he would seek Paul's prayers on their behalf (ch. 43). He then saw Christ visiting the dead as they waited in their prison. Christ told him that because of Michael and Paul, and their own sons who had kept the commandments, He would give them rest (ch. 44).

The descent of Christ into the world of the spirits is mentioned in the New Testament in 1 Peter 3:18-22 and 1 Peter 4:6. By the end of the first century it was a well-accepted notion and became widespread thereafter. Irenaeus (130-200) quoted an elder of the Church as follows:

> The Lord descended into the regions beneath the earth, preaching His advent there also and the remission of sins received by those who believe in Him.[23]

Both Irenaeus and Justin Martyr (100-165) quote from the Apocryphon of Jeremiah a text as follows:

> The Lord God remembered His dead, the saints of Israel that have fallen asleep in the dust of the tomb, and He went down unto them to proclaim the good news of the salvation which he was bringing to them.[24]

The Shepherd of Hermas speaks of a baptism for these departed souls and Clement of Alexandria (150-215), after referring to Hermas, extended that salvation to the gentiles as well as the ancient Israelite prophets.[25]

The theme of Christ's descent into hell to preach to and save the spirits there is found also in the Epistle of the Apostles 26-27; the Testaments of the Twelve Patriarchs (Levi iv:1; Dan v. 10-11; Benjamin ix:5), the Ascension of Isaiah (ix:16-17); the Sybilline Oracles (viii:310-312); the Odes of Solomon (xvii:8-11). Origen (225) taught that the prophets and John the Baptist continued their earthly ministries into the spirit world with the dead. He also taught that Moses and Elijah, following their visitation to Jesus and the three apostles on the Mount of Transfiguration, returned to the world of the dead and proclaimed to them what they had just experienced.[26] By the third century of Christianity, it was common for authors to discuss John the Baptist entering hell before Jesus to prepare the way for him there, just as he had in his earthly life.[27]

The Muslim tradition is quite familiar with the ascension motif. As already stated, the Qur'ān (6:76) refers to God bringing Abraham up to the vault of heaven. Muhammed (as well as several others before him) is said to have ascended up to the seventh heaven. The Qur'ān, however, barely mentions it. In 17:1 it refers to a night journey that the prophet took to Jerusalem, but says nothing of an ascension. A number of other verses imply that Muhammed's enemies (and certainly, therefore, his friends) knew of such an experience, however, for Allāh tells Muhammed to challenge them to ascend to heaven if they can (52.38). His enemies are represented as saying to him:

> We will not put faith in thee till thou . . . ascend up into heaven and even then we will put no faith in thine ascension till thou bring down for us a book that we can read. (17:90-93)

About one hundred years after the death of Muhammed, Ibn-Ishaq (702-768) wrote a biography of the Prophet (the *Sirat Rasul Allāh*). Within this biography is a detailed account of the ascension. One night as the Prophet lay asleep in Mecca, the angel Gabriel visited him, and together they traveled to Jerusalem to the temple. There the Prophet found several of the ancient prophets (Abraham, Moses, Jesus) whom he led in prayer. After this, Gabriel took Muhammed to heaven. Ascending upon a ladder (Arabic: *miraj,* the word used for ascension), Muhammed visited each of the seven heavens, which were presided over by former prophets: Adam in the first, reviewing the spirits as they entered; Jesus and John the Baptist in the second; Joseph in the third; Enoch in the fourth; Aaron in the fifth; Moses in the sixth; and Abraham in the seventh. From there Muhammed was led to the gates of Paradise wherein Allāh Himself resided. Muhammed held an interview with God, who commanded him to recite prayers regularly and to teach his followers to do likewise.[28]

A later writer, Ibn S'ad (800-862), wrote a narrative of the world's history from Adam to Muhammed, a sort of Biblical commentary, entitled *Kitab al-tibaqat al kabir*. He related the experience of the ascension as outlined above. He added that

Gabriel was accompanied by Michael, and that during the night this ascension took place, Muhammed's relatives found his body missing from its bed and looked for him. This suggests that for Muhammed, at least, the experience was "in the body" and not out of it.[29]

Recently J. R. Porter has discussed this night journey and has found in the various accounts of it elements similar to shamanism. Certain elements of the shaman's call to practice his profession are common to the accounts of Muhammed's experience and suggest that this ascent may have been undertaken at the very beginning of his calling. For instance, Muhammed spoke with former prophets, as a shaman will speak with former shamans and ancestors, who were also often shamans. The use of the ladder also has shamanistic functions and is to be found in several other ascension examples, e.g., Jacob and Buddha. The ladder is referred to by Muhammed as that which the dead look for upon dying. This relates the experience to shamanism, because one of the major functions of the shaman is to seek out the soul of the dead or sick person, which is believed to have been taken away by spirits. Further evidence that this ascension constitutes the calling of Muhammed to be a prophet is that each of the prophets which met in the heavens asked Gabriel if Muhammed had received a calling yet. These and other considerations lead Porter to conclude that "Muhammed's journey to the other world is not just a late invention of pious fancy but is rather an essential part of his prophetic call."[30]

Indian thought is often portrayed as being monistic, with man eventually merging or fusing himself into the One and losing all identity. Such a belief leaves little room for theism, yet from the very earliest times there has been a strong theistic current running through Hinduism. From the Svetasvatara Upanishad to the present day, the Indian has sought for and found fulfillment in worshipping his individual god. Even Sankara (A.D. 788-820), the greatest monistic philosopher of India, practiced theism to a certain degree, with many theistic texts credited to him.

While mysticism and ecstatic experiences are well known in India, texts dealing primarily with ascension motifs are not. Stories of saints and seers who possess the ability to pass from this world to the next without any problem are current from the earliest periods of Indian literature. Determining the historicity of some of these seers is virtually impossible in many cases. The ascension experiences themselves are used little by later writers. For instance, in Judeo-Christian-Muslim thought much is made of the experiences of the early patriarchs and prophets — entire volumes being written about the apocalypse or ascension of such an individual. In India this did not occur. Consequently detailing such experiences is much more difficult.

The experience referred to in the western world as translation — such as experienced by Enoch and Elijah — is known in India. For instance, just two hundred years ago Tukaram was caught up by a flaming chariot and carried into heaven rather than undergoing the change known as death.[31] Long before Tukaram, however, Yudhisthira, the oldest of the five Pandava brothers, had a similar experience. At the end of his life, as recorded in the Mahabharata, he and his brothers were ascending to heaven. One by one the younger four fell away and died because of some minor sin each had committed. Even Yudhisthira underwent changes as he progressed closer to heaven. After arriving there, he was given a vision of hell and its tortures.[32]

The oldest literature of India are the Vedas. These are the hymns sung during the rituals of Hinduism and as such, they are little disposed to relate personal occurrences of humans. There are two hymns, however, that seem to refer to ascension experiences of human beings. The first is in Rig Veda 7.88.3ff. This is an account of the ancient sage Vasistha, who enters the underworld governed by Lord Varuna. He enters that otherworld on a boat, which is a common theme for ascensions. As a result of this experience he became a seer, *rsi*. The other account is equally nebulous. This is the famous Kesin hymn ("Long haired one") found in Rig Veda 10.136.1ff. Kesin describes himself as being lifted to the wind and sailing through the air. While no account is given of actually being carried into heaven or the underworld, it would appear to be similar to many other accounts wherein the individual merely views the earth from above.

There is one ascension experience, however, which fits very well the pattern found in the other accounts. That experience belongs to Arjuna, one of the younger brothers of Yudhisthira and the hero of the Mahabharata. Arjuna was seeking to secure the divine weapons of the gods in order to protect himself and his brothers from their enemies. He walked northward to the Himalayas, where he practiced the ascetic life. The different deities did come and present their own weapons to him. Then Matali, the divine charioteer, descended. Arjuna purified himself in the Ganges, repeated his prayers, gratified the ancestral fathers (*pitrs*), and then invoked Mandara, the mountain which figured as an axis mundi during the Churning of the Ocean (during the war between the *devas* and *asuras*). He then mounted the chariot and ascended with Matali to heaven. On their way they passed many heroes who had died in battle (doing their duty as warriors), ascetics, and other minor deities, all of whom Matali described as "virtuous persons."

"Having thus passed through successive regions of heaven [Arjuna] at last" arrived at the palace of Indra, the supreme deity in heaven.

> The region was such that none could behold it who had not gone through ascetic austerities, or who had not poured libations on fire. It was a region for the virtuous alone, [a region for those] who had . . . bathed in sacred waters, . . . [who possessed] a knowledge of the Vedas.

Arjuna then saw Indra himself, who immediately embraced Arjuna and invited him to share half of his own throne. Arjuna thereupon began to blaze forth like a second Indra. The other deities of heaven washed his feet. He then received Indra's *vajra* or thunderbolt. With this *vajra* he was sent out to defeat in battle the *asuras* (*nivata kavachas* or *danavas*), just as Indra himself had defeated all his enemies in the mythical past. Having spent five years in Indraloka, Arjuna descended.[33]

Early Buddhism is the area of Indian thought where much more is said about ascension. There is a tradition in the literature of early Buddhism relating that four *bhikkhus* had ascended bodily into heaven and remained there for some time. These four were: Sadhina and Mandhata, each of whom ruled for some length of time in heaven; Nimi, who spent seven days viewing heaven and hell; and Guttila, a musician who spent seven days visiting the inhabitants of heaven. All four are described as being earlier incarnations of the Bodhisatta (the Buddha before his last life when he gained his enlightenment and became known as the Buddha).[34]

In the Uposatha sutta of the Anguttara nikaya (2.183), the Buddha stated that some monks are capable of gaining access to the world of the *devas* and the Brahmas. One of those monks who gained such access was Anuruddha (who along with Moggallana, Mahakassapa, and Mahakappina, ascended into the Brahma loka to correct the false pride of one of the inhabitants thereof). In a discourse of his own, Anuruddha explains to the monks that one may gain the ability to ascend into another world by cultivating the four *satipatthanas*. He explains this in the Iddhi sutta of the samyutta nikaya (5.303). The four *satipatthanas,* or "mindfulnesses," are explained in a discourse of the Buddha, found in the Majjhima nikaya (sutta 10; Digha nikaya, discourse 22). The Buddha taught that there is one way (*ekayano maggo*) for the purification of beings, for the extinction of unhappiness and depression, for the acquisition of right method, and for the realization of nirvana. That one way is the cultivation of the four *satipatthanas*. One must eliminate both desire and aversion for the world with reference to the body, the sensations of the body, one's mental thoughts, and the phenomena of the world (*dharma*). One does this by removing the five obstacles (*nivārana*), which are stated to be one's internal will to pleasure, malevolence, stupidity, vanity (or the desire to do things which will bring praise from others), and uncertainty or doubt. The fruit of such activity will be either *annā* here or the gaining of the status of *anāgāmin*. *Annā* is a technical term which is perhaps best translated by the Greek word *gnosis*. It is that knowledge which is more sure, more real, more true, which is based on experience and not syllogistic reasoning. It is a witness which one gains, and which the monks and nuns shared in their poems contained in the Theragatha and Therigatha texts.[35] The *anāgāmin* is that individual who has been assured that, while he has not gained full liberation in this life, he will gain it during his life as a *deva* in the next world.

Moggallana was one of the favorite disciples (along with his one personal friend Sariputta). Moggallana was known for his many visits to the heavenly kingdoms, the vast majority of which are contained in one volume, the *Vimanavatthu*. In most of these stories Moggallana is merely interested in determining what it was by virtue of which the individual was raised to the status of a *deva* or god following his demise in this world. The *Vimanavatthu* is a rather late addition to the Pali canon. That the stories may have significant basis for inclusion is evident, however, from some stories related about Moggallana in what are definitely earlier texts.

In the Anguttara Nikaya of the Suttapitaka, there is an account of a visit which Moggallana paid to Tissa, a former monk who had died and been reborn in Brahmaloka. Upon recognizing him Tissa said, "It is long since you made this round, I mean, come here." This early text indicates that Moggallana already had a reputation for being able to ascend to the other worlds. There are four accounts in the Nikayas of Moggallana ascending in order to determine how it was that the individual had been born where he was.[36] A fifth account details another visit he paid to Tissa in the Brahmaloka. Tissa indicates to him that anyone who is satisfied with the life he is living in the Brahmaloka will remain there. If one desires to progress beyond that heavenly kingdom, however, he must not be satisfied, but must gain the knowledge that will project him beyond the Brahmaloka, which is the highest of the seven Buddhist heavens.[37]

The Buddha himself visited the heavens on several occasions. In the Ayogula sutta[38] the Buddha tells Ananda, his beloved disciple, that he, Buddha, can ascend with his physical body into the Brahmaloka. He can do this by applying certain meditative powers to his mind, by means of which his body becomes radiant and plastic. In such a condition his body lifts off the ground and ascends.[39] The first person to whom Buddha explained his enlightenment was Upaka, who also became the first to reject the Buddha's testimony.[40] After dying, Upaka was reborn in one of the Brahmalokas where the Buddha visited him and taught him. Upaka soon became an *arahant*, "perfected one," and achieved nirvana.[41]

Another text recounts a visit the Buddha paid to the *devas* residing in a particular Brahmaloka (there are several kingdoms within the Brahma world).[42] On another occasion the Buddha visited Bakabrahma in the Brahmaloka, where they discussed the eternality of individuals.[43]

The most famous ascension of the Buddha, however, came during the seventh year following his enlightenment. With three strides he ascended to the Tavatimsa heaven, there to spend three months teaching the devas assembled, including his mother who had died when he was just an infant. He taught while seated upon Sakka's throne, just as Arjuna had sat on it. It was during this time that Sariputta visited him daily, in order to receive instructions of what to teach the disciples on earth. When it came time to return to earth, a ladder was placed from heaven to earth at Sankassa. The god Sakka descended on his left side, Brahma on his right. A shrine was built at the site, which was still there several hundred years later when the Chinese pilgrims Hiouen Thsang and Fa Hien visited it.[44]

When one interprets the religious experiences of a religious tradition other than one's own, one must be extremely careful not to let his own attitudes interfere or corrupt. Cultures and cultural symbols differ, and therefore the interpretations of those symbols may be different. To interpret a given symbol from another culture in terms of the interpretation given for that symbol in one's own tradition may be to interpret incorrectly. Worse yet, it may perhaps lead to confusion and ignorance, which in turn may lead to prejudice. Sympathy and understanding are needed. Professor Kees Bolle, in making some remarks on Bhakti, a form of Hindu religious worship, has stated:

> A sympathetic attitude on the part of the investigator is of course indispensable, but the investigation into a religion other than the investigator's must show not only sympathy, but also understanding. Otherwise a study reveals more of the student than of the subject studied. The nature of the student's speculation on the universality of religious experience may be interesting, but it should tally with an empirical research. In other words, he should not force his own ideas or the structures of his own culture on the culture that he studies in order to make his speculation acceptable.[45]

But more than sympathy and understanding are necessary. When dealing with religious experience, one must be willing to admit that such experience is actually a possibility; otherwise one's personal bias regarding that experience will cloud the interpretation of it. One will be required to seek other reasons for the explanation of that experience.

Fazlur Rahman, in his volume on Islam in the *History of Religions* series, has written that Muhammed's ascension experience "developed by the orthodox (chiefly on the pattern of the Ascension of Jesus) and backed by Hadith [tradition] is no more than a historical fiction whose materials come from various sources."[46] Rahman has here shown perhaps more of his own attitude toward the possibility of an ascension experience than he has of the experience itself.

Another attitude toward the ascension experience is that given by G. H. Box, the translator of several early apocryphal texts. In the introduction to his translation of the Apocalypse of Abraham he wrote:

> The mystic who is allowed to enter the celestial sphere usually receives divine disclosures about the future of the spiritual world. In order to enjoy this experience the mystic has to prepare himself to enter the ecstatic state which is brought about especially by ablution and fasting, but also sometimes by fervent invocations.[47]

Here Professor Box does not give his own beliefs as to the possibility of an ascension experience, but neither does he assign it to the realm of historical fiction or try to relate it to some ritual activity. He is content to speak of it in terms which the author of the text himself has put it.

There are several functions for the ascension experience. On the one hand, it is obviously for the benefit of the individual who is taken into heaven or hell. It is meant to be a guide for the individual in his newly consecrated life, as a prophet or a shaman, or, as in the case of the North American Indian, simply for guiding him throughout his life, giving him an understanding of his own place in the cosmos. As the Koran stated in regard to Abraham, it is for the purpose of allowing him to "possess certainty." The same was true for the Buddhist theory of ascension, wherein uncertainty or doubt was the last of the obstacles to be removed — the removal of which gave one that *anna* or *gnosis*.

On the other hand, it is for the purpose of the individual before he dies. It is to allow him to depart without sorrow (Abraham); to see the reward of the pious or the sufferings of the wicked (Moses); to see his own throne prepared for him (Moses); or for the individual simply to die in peace (Box and Kohler, quoting Midrashim).

There are several similarities that find their way into some of the experiences found throughout the world. Among these is the idea that there are several heavens (and hells), not just one. These heavens are actual places in which living people dwell; they are not just various levels of the firmament. As one progresses upward, one is confronted with brighter and brighter lights. To compensate for this light, which at times becomes blinding so as to prevent one from seeing properly, the individual must change form, or be given special garments which protect him, or have his vision changed into a "heavenly vision" that permits him to see without being blinded.

Another element common to many of the texts is that there is life after death, and that life is a conscious, active life. One's soul or spirit does not rest asleep during that next life. Further, there is progress to be made during that life. In short, death is not the end of life but rather a new beginning; it is merely a change of scenery.

There is a third function for the ascension, besides those of personal benefit in one's life and for aiding the individual in preparing for death and the life to come. That third function will perhaps be best understood by reference to the ritual ascension motif. After a lengthy study of the motif as found in the ancient Near East, primarily pre-Muslim Arabic sources, George Widengren gives the following statement regarding an ideal ritual ascension:

> We may arrive at the 'ideal' ritual of the heavenly ascent . . . after the following pattern:
> (1.) The ascent to heaven
> (2.) The presentation before God
> (3.) The clothing in a garment and the adorning
> (4.) The crowning with a crown

(5.) The calling by name, i.e. the proclamation as the Elect and the Beloved
(6.) The enthronement on God's own seat
(7.) The gift of knowledge of God's own doing
(8.) The communion by drinking from God's own cup
(9.) The union with God, i.e. the elevation to the divine state
(10.) The return with a special commission.[48]

There is in ancient Indian sources a ritual performed by the king that has several of the elements mentioned by Widengren, but which at any rate is a ritual ascension. This is the rajasuya ceremony, which was recently studied by J. C. Heesterman. He writes:

> It is explicitly stated that it is to be performed by a king who wants to obtain access to heaven (svargakama). The rajasuya seems to have been originally a yearly repeated rite of cosmic regeneration and rebirth.[49]

The *rajasuya* is without doubt an ascension ritually accomplished. The very first element of it is the *prayaniya,* a term which translates into ascension. (Heesterman, 12-3) The king is clothed in sacred garments ("The garment is connected with all the gods," says an ancient text); the garments are said to be marked in special ways, representative of the ceremony undertaken by the king.[50] The garment consists of several parts, one of which is worn on the head (Widengren's crown), the ends of which are tied into the upper garment.[51] Throughout the ritual the king is called by the name of the various gods whom he is impersonating. He is taken back into primordial time and performs the same functions symbolically which the gods and the first king did at that time, by virtue of which *they* obtained heaven.[52] The king is then enthroned on a throne which is addressed as being the navel of kingship and the cosmos.

> The throne represents the center, the navel of the earth. . . . It combines the notions of the navel and birthplace of the world and the king with those of the central mountain.[53]

The king is given God's special knowledge in the form of learning those things which occurred in *illo tempore,* which lead to the gods becoming that which they have become.

An interesting tale is related to the king about an ancient Vedic seer named Sunahsepa. Sunahsepa was tied to a sacrificial pillar, about to be sacrified. He cried out for help, seeking for new parents (his only earthly parents were responsible for his being sold as a sacrificial victim). God Varuna heard his pleas and released him from the fetters which bound him. The message of the story is a genealogical one: to whom does Sunahsepa belong? Who are his real father and mother? The *rajasuya* is also concerned with ancestry, as well as the future offspring of the king.[54] The king, continuing with the ritual, drinks the same draft of *soma* which Indra had when he was called to defeat the *assuras* in the primordial war in heaven. According to an ancient text, the *rajasuya,* in Gonda's words, is a process of ''deification''.[55] This fulfills Widengren's contention regarding the elevation to the divine state. The king then descends, the king and the world regenerated and reborn.

It is evident that the ritual ascension as exemplified in the *rajasuya* is for the benefit of the king following this life. It may be of regenerative value for the here and now, both for the king and for his subjects, which actually include the entire earth, but its major function, as indicated, is for the king to attain heaven following death.

In the Mahabharata, an ancient Indian epic, it also has another function. Narada, an ancient Vedic *rishi* or seer, was coursing through the heavenly worlds, visiting the various levels of heaven and discoursing with the inhabitants therein. He describes the various heavens and the people who inhabit them. He then visits the lowest heaven, that of the *pitrs,* or fathers, the ancestors of those then living on earth. One of those *pitrs* was a former king named Pandu. He had a special request to make of Narada. If Narada were to meet with his five sons when he returned to the earth, would he please ask those sons to perform the *rajasuya* in behalf of their father? If they would, said Pandu, then he would be enabled to advance to the highest heaven wherein Indra dwells. Upon encountering the five sons of Pandu, Narada stated:

> If thou performest that sacrifice thou shall then be able to go, along with thy deceased ancestors, into the same region that is inhabited by the chief of the immortals [Indra].[56]

The Pandavas, the five sons of Pandu of whom the Mahabharata is the personal story, then perform that sacrifice in behalf of their dead ancestor.

It is evident from this account that the *rajasuya,* while being primarily a ritual for the benefit of the living, can be, if performed accordingly, a ritual in behalf of one's ancestors. In other words, it has vicarious value, as well as value for the living. It is this aspect which becomes the third function of the ascension motif. In almost all of the ascension experiences studied in this paper, the vicarious element has entered, however slight. In the case of Jesus, it obviously had greater place. The sole purpose of Jesus descending into hell was to teach the inhabitants and release them from their bondage so that they might gain access to heaven. Origen, writing during the first half of the third century A.D., implied that the prophets before Jesus (i.e., the Old Testament prophets) up to and including John the Baptist, after finishing their earthly ministries, resumed those ministries when entering the world of the dead. He also indicated that Moses and Elijah, following their visit with Jesus and the three apostles on the Mount of Transfiguration, returned to the spirit world and told the inhabitants there that the Advent was soon to take place.[57] Enoch, following his translation into heaven, had spent his days teaching the children who died in infancy;[58] Abraham prayed that the dead might receive a better judgment, and his prayer was effective; Moses saw the angel teaching in the "college on high" and was told that the pious son would save the unrighteous father; Paul was told that if he and his angel guide, Michael, would pray, it would benefit the dead; Muhammed ascended into heaven on a ladder, just as the dead do; the Buddha ascended into the *tavatimsa* heaven for the sole purpose of teaching his mother who had died when he was just seven days old and therefore had not heard the gospel her son was proclaiming on earth; the shaman receives his ascension calling so that he might learn the secrets of regaining the souls of those who are sick and/or dead. All of these experiences reveal, in greater or lesser detail, that the living can indeed be of benefit to their dead ancestors. This would seem to be one of the prime reasons for the ascension of the individual and his writing down the account.

Whatever the reason for God calling an individual into heaven, and the purpose of this paper is not to imply that vicarious salvation is the only reason, that reason must relate to the personal integrity of the individual. It is also an experience which has singular benefit for the individual, an experience not to be lightly treated or spoken of.[59] As indicated of Abraham, it is an experience to give one "certainty," or as in the case of the Buddha, to remove all uncertainty or doubt. The individual is given a knowledge to sustain him throughout his earthly life. It must be one of the most exquisite and soul-inspiring messages written deep on the heart and mind of the righteous who is entitled to such an experience. Perhaps the best means of expressing the value of the experience is by quoting the words of Joseph Smith in the Doctrine and Covenants. Section 76 relates his own vision in which he was shown the condition of those in hell, as well as the various levels or kingdoms making up heaven:

> But great and marvelous are the works of the Lord, and the mysteries of his kingdom which he showed unto us, which surpass all understanding in glory, and in might, and in dominion; Which he commanded us we should not write while we were yet in the Spirit, and are not lawful for man to utter; Neither is man capable to make them known, for they are only to be seen and understood by the power of the Holy Spirit, which God bestows on those who love him, and purify themselves before him; To whom he grants this privilege of seeing and knowing for themselves; That through the power and manifestation of the Spirit, while in the flesh, they may be able to bear his presence in the world of glory. (D&C 76:114-118)

NOTES

1. Quoted in Frits Staal, *Exploring Mysticism* (Penguin Books, 1975), p. 65. Diogenes is perhaps best known as the individual who walked about Athens in broad daylight with a lantern, looking for an honest man. He lived during the fourth century B.C.

2. Joseph Fielding Smith, *Teachings of the Prophet Joseph Smith* (Salt Lake City: Deseret Book, 1964), p. 160 (hereafter cited as *TPJS);* Joseph Smith, *Documentary History of the Church,* 6:50; cf. John Taylor, *Messenger and Advocate* (June 1837): 513-14.

3. Mircea Eliade, *Rites and Symbols of Initiation* (New York: Harper Torchbooks, 1958), p. 78.

4. Jean Danielou, *The Theology of Jewish Christianity* (Chicago: Henry Rennerylo, 1964), p. 253.

5. G. H. Box, introduction to the *Testament of Abraham,* trans. G. H. Box (London: Society for Promoting Christian Knowledge, 1927), p. xviii, referring to K. Kohler, "The Apocalypse of Abraham and Its Kindred," in *Jewish Quarterly Review* (July 1895), p. 593.

6. Cf. Mircea Eliade, *Shamanism* (Princeton, New Jersey: Princeton University Press, 1974), pp. 252-53, 259-60.

7. H. Wheeler Robinson, "The Council of Yahweh," in *Journal of Theological Studies* 14 (1944) :152.

8. Patrick Miller, *The Divine Warrior in Early Israel* (Cambridge, Massachusetts: Harvard, 1973), pp. 68-69. In the first and second chapters of the Book of Job there is a description of such a divine assembly, wherein "the sons of God came to present themselves before the Lord." A discussion follows, and Job is picked as a subject of divine activity. H. Wheeler Robinson, in the article cited above, states that this picture of the assembly "is to be taken seriously" ("The Council of Yahweh," p. 153). In later Hebrew mythology the same scene is repeated, with the same participants, except that the discussion is about Abraham rather than Job. The discussion resulted in the offering of Isaac by his father, Abraham. Cf. Sanhedrin, 89b, in Angelo Rappoport, *Myth and Legend of Ancient Israel* (Ktav Pub, 1966), 1:286-7. Cf. R. N. Whybray, *The Heavenly Counselor in Isaiah xl 13-14* (Cambridge, England: Cambridge University Press, 1971), pp. 49-53.

9. George Widengren, in his exhaustive study of the Prophet Muhammed, draws attention to the first three chapters of Ezekiel wherein the calling of Ezekiel to be a prophet is described. "It is important to note," writes Widengren, "that the event is enacted in heaven before the throne of God." (*The Ascension of the Apostle and the Heavenly Book* [Uppsala Universitets Arsskrift, 1950], 7:31.) Ezekiel

describes the sights and sounds which he sensed on that occasion: the hosts of heaven, the voice of the Almighty, the throne above the heads of the hosts, the color of that throne; and then the words of God to him as he is "sent out" to Israel to call her to repentance. Again, in the calling of Isaiah to be a prophet we read the same things: he sees the Lord sitting upon his throne, with his assembly members about him (the seraphim). One of these seraphim comes to Isaiah and purifies his mouth with a hot coal so that he will be worthy to stand in the presence of that assembly. He hears God asking whom shall he send. Isaiah volunteers and is sent out as a prophet.

10. Testament of Levi 5.1, in R. H. Charles, *Pseudepigrapha of the Old Testament,* 1913, p. 307; *Pirke de Rabbi Eliezer,* trans. Gerald Friedlander (New York: Hermion Press, 1964 [1916]), p. 184; cf. Ginzberg, *Legends of the Jews,* 1:387; 2:194-98.

11. Book of Mormon, 1 Nephi 1:4-20. The Book of Mormon is among those books which S. G. F. Brandon designates as Holy Books, in the "The Holy Book, the Holy Tradition and the Holy Ikon, A Phenomenological Survey," in F. F. Bruce and E. G. Rupp, eds. *Holy Book and Holy Tradition* (Manchester University Press, 1968), p. 2. In his discussion of those books which have at one time or another been seriously or otherwise considered as claiming a position in the Christian canon, M. R. James includes the Book of Mormon. M. R. James, *The Apocryphal New Testament,* (Oxford: The Clarendon Press, 1966), p. xviii.

12. On Adam, see Ginzberg, *Legends of the Jews,* 1:84: Seth, see Rappoport, *Myth and Legend of Ancient Israel,* 1:201; on Enoch, see the various Books of Enoch, also Ginzberg, *Legends of the Jews,* 1:130ff; 5:96, 163, 165; Ginzberg states that "the older rabbinic literature is not particularly favorably inclined toward Enoch." 5:96, note 67. On Isaac, see Ginzberg, 1:286, 306; 5:254, 263. On Jacob, see Ginzberg, 1:350ff; Rappoport 1:347-8; Altman, *Jewish Quarterly Review* 35 (1945):390; Hugh Nibley, "Christian Envy of the Temple," in *Jewish Quarterly Review,* 50, note 129; Joseph Smith, in *TPJS*, pp. 304-5. On Jeremiah, see Ginzberg 6:400; 5:95-6. On Baruch, see Ginzberg, 4:323.

13. Midrash Rabbah xliv 12 (on Genesis 15:5); *Apocalypse of Abraham* G. H. Box, trans. (Society for Promoting Christian Knowledge, 1918), xii, xv; *Testament of Abraham,* trans. by C. H. Box, 1927, and by Michael E. Stone, chapter ixf. Cf. IV Ezra iii.14; Philo, Biblical Antiquities, xviii; Apocalypse of Baruch 4.4.

14. *Apocalypse of Abraham.*

15. *Testament of Abraham*. Cf. Kohler, *Jewish Quarterly Review*, 1893, and Ginzberg; and Rappoport 1:327-35.

16. Ginzberg, 5: 416-17.

17. M. Gaster, "Hebrew Visions of Hell and Paradise," in *Journal of the Royal Asiatic Society (JRAS)* (1893), p. 579.

18. Gaster, "Hebrew Visions of Hell and Paradise," p. 587; Ginzberg 2: 314-15.

19. Ginzberg 3: 109-17.

20. Midrash Rabbah on Deuteronomy xi. 7-10.

21. Midrash Rabbah 4: 185.

22. Book of the Resurrection of Christ by Bartholomew the Apostle, in M. R. James, *Apocryphal New Testament*, p. 184, says that all the apostles went up to the seventh heaven. Hippolytus, commenting on Daniel 4:60, states that Jesus took all the apostles to Paradise (p. 37); Siophanes, the son of the apostle Thomas, stated that he had an "out-of-the-body experience" in which Michael took his soul up to heaven, where he saw the twleve thrones for the apostles (p. 185).

23. Irenaeus, Adv. Haer. iv. 27:2, quoted from Danielou, *The Theology of Jewish Christianity*, p. 235.

24. Irenaeus, Adv. Haer. iii. 20.4; iv. 22.1; 33.1; 33.12; v. 31.1; Dem. 78; Justin Martyr, Dial, lxxii.4; in Danielou, *The Theology of Jewish Christianity, p. 235.*

25. Shepherd of Hermas, Similitudes 9.15.5-7; Clement, Stromateis ii. 43. 5; vi. 45.4.

26. "Moses and Elijah, having appeared in glory and talked with Jesus, went away to the place from which they had come, perhaps to communicate the words which Jesus spake with them, to those who were to be benefitted by Him, almost immediately namely at the time of the passion, when many of the bodies of the saints that had fallen asleep, their tombs being opened, were to go to the city which is truly holy . . . and there appear to many." Origen, "Commentary on the Gospel of Matthew, trans. John Patrick, in *Ante-Nicene Fathers*, 9: 473. Cf. Daniel Sheerin, "St. John the Baptist in the Lower World," in *Vigiliae Christianae* 30 (March 1976): 4.

27. See Sheerin, "St. John the Baptist in the Lower World"; Danielou, *The Theology of Jewish Christianity;* also Jean Danielou, *The Work of John the Baptist* (Baltimore: Helison, 1966), p. 147; Sirarpie der Nersessian, "A Homily on the Raising of Lazarus and the Harrowing of Hell," in *Biblical and Patristic Studies in Memory of R. P. Casey*, pp. 224-25.

28. *The Life of Muhammed,* trans. A. Guillaume (Oxford, England: Oxford University Press, 1955), pp. 181-87; J. R. Porter, "Muhammed's Journey to Heaven," in *Numen* 21 (1974): 64-66.

29. Trans. by S. Moinul Haq (Karachi: Pakistan Historical Society, 1967), pp. 246-49.

30. Porter, "Muhammed's Journey to Heaven"; cf. K. Wagtendonk, *Fasting in the Koran* (Leiden: E. J. Brill, 1968), pp. 110-11.

31. Mahipati, *Bhaktalilamrta,* trans. Justin Abbott (1930), pp. 312-13.

32. *The Mahabharata,* trans. Pratap Chandra Roy (Calcutta: n.d.). Mahaprasthanka parva, section II, vol. XI: 271-75; Svargarohanika parva, vol. XI: 278-82.

33. *Mahabharata,* Vanaparva (Indralokagamana parva), trans. Roy, vol. II: 99-108; 354-70.

34. See Jatakas numbers 494, 258, 541, 243. There are several other stories in early Buddhist literature regarding individuals who ascended into heaven for short periods of time: Dhatarattha, a mythical king (Jataka vi. 251); Nārada, an ancient seer, who is prominent in the Mahabharata (Sudhabhojana jataka, no. 535); Ajita, a seer who heard a commotion in heaven, and upon investigating, discovered that the Buddha had just been born and the inhabitants of heaven were rejoicing (Nidana katha, introduction to the Jataka text); Silavatī, an ancient queen, who visited Tavatimsa, where Sakka or Indra rules (George Malalasekera, *Dictionary of Pali Proper Names* [London: John Murray, 1937], 1: 1003); a monk who wishes to know where all the elements pass away and goes to the various heavens in order to find the answer (Kevaddha suttanta, in Digha nikaya, discourse xi); Nanda, who was carried aloft by the Buddha himself (Sangamavacarat Jataka; Udana iii.2); Sariputta, one of the favorite disciples, who visited Buddha daily while the latter was visiting there for three months (in Malalasekera, *Dictionary of Pali Proper Names* 1: 795); Labhibhū, who went to Brahmaloka with Sikkhi Buddha, an earlier Buddha (arunavati sitta, in Samyutta Nikaya 5.282-4).

35. N. T. W. Rhys Davids and William Stede, *The Pali Text Society's Pali-English Dictionary* (Luzac and Co., 1959), p. 14, uses the word *gnosis* as a possible translation. The Sanskrit form is *ājnā,* from the verb *Jnā,* which Monier-Williams' *Sanskrit English Dictionary,* Oxford, also translates as gnosis under two of the related words, pp. 425-26.

36. Anguttara nikaya iii. 331-32; Samyutta nikaya v. 366-69.

37. Anguttara nikaya iv. 75-8.

38. Samyutta nikaya v. 282-84.

39. The Pali Buddhist term for ascension is *devacārikā*, "coursing in the deva worlds."

40. Vinaya pitaka i. 8; Majjhima nikaya i. 170-71; Jataka i. 81.

41. Samyutta nikaya i. 35, 60.

42. Digha nikaya ii. 50-52, the Mahapadana sutta.

43. Bakabrahma sutta, Samyutta nikaya i. 142. Cf. Baka Brahma jataka, no. 405; aparaditthi sutta, samyutta nikaya i. 144.

44. Malalasekera, *Dictionary of Pali Proper Names,* subj.: Sankassa, Gotama; tavatimsa. Fa Hien, *Record of Buddhistic Kingdoms,* trans. James Legge, pp. 47-51, 68. Sakka is generally identified with Indra.

45. Kees W. Bolle, "Remarks on Bhakti," *Adyar Library Bulletin 25* (December 1960): p. 116.

46. Fazlur Rahman, *Islam* (New York: Holt, Rinehart and Winston, 1966), p. 14. Compare Porter's statement above.

47. G. H. Box, introduction to *Apocalypse of Abraham,* p. xxix.

48. George Widengren, *Muhammed, the Apostle of God and His Ascension* (Uppsala: Universitets Arsskrift, 1955), p. 92.

49. J. C. Heesterman, *The Ancient Indian Royal Consecration; the rajasuya described according to the Yajus texts and annotated* (The Hague: Mouton and Co., 1957), p. 7.

50. Ibid., pp. 97-98, 105 note 7, 170.

51. Ibid., p. 92.

52. Ibid., pp. 13, 67, 127-39.

53. Ibid., p. 149.

54. Ibid., 159-60, 184; on offspring, 190, 201-202; on the Sunahsepa legend, see H. L. Hariyappa, "The Legend of Sunahsepa," *Bulletin of Deccan College Research Institute* (Poona) 11 (1951): 123-330.

55. Taittiriya Brahmana 1.1.6.8, in Jans Gonda, *Ancient Indian Kingship,* p. 86.

56. Mahabharata II (Sabha parvan), trans. Roy, i. 481.

57. Origen, "Commentary on the Gospel of Matthew," trans. John Patrick, in *Ante-Nicene Fathers,* 9: 473.

58. Jerusalem Talmud, Abodah Zorah 3b.

59. Rabbi Aher "cut the plants," i.e. made bad use of his learning when, having been admitted within paradise, he "went forth into evil courses." Elijah told Rabbi Bar Shila that God did not utter doctrine by the mouth of Rabbi Meir because he had learned it from the mouth of Rabbi A'her. *Babylonian Talmud,* Hagiga, trans. M. L. Rodkinson, 1918, 5: 33.

Reverence for Life in Religion: Eastern and Western Views

5

Gerald E. Jones

Ahimsa is an Eastern term referring to a reverence for life which implies non-injury to any living thing. It is based on a belief that sacred and divine powers undergird all natural or physical forms. The Jains, followers of Nataputta Vardhamana, best known as Mahavira, (c. 600 B.C.), are the most noted disciples of respect for all living creatures. The "Pillow of Righteousness" sutra recounts Mahavira's teachings on ahimsa:

> Thoroughly knowing the earth-bodies and fire-bodies and wind-bodies, the lichens, seeds, and sprouts,
>
> He comprehended that they are if narrowly inspected, imbued with life, and avoided to injure them. (1:xi-xii)
>
> Practising the sinless abstinence from killing. (1:xvi)
>
> In Ladha . . . the dogs bit him [and] ran at him. (3:iii)
>
> Few people kept off the attacking, biting dogs. Striking the monk, they cried "khukkhu" and made the dogs bite him. (3:iv)
>
> Ceasing to use the stick against living beings, abandoning the care of the body, the houseless Mahavira, the Venerable One, endures the thornes of the villages perfectly enlightened. (3:vii)

> Without ceasing in his reflections . . . the Venerable One slowly wandered about, and, killing no creatures, he begged for his food. (4:xii)[1]

This practice was later codified in the first of Five Great Vows' for Jain monks.

> I renounce all killing of living beings, whether subtile or gross . . . Nor shall I myself kill living beings.
>
> A Nirgrantha [monk] is careful in his walk, not careless. The Kevalin assigns as the reason, that a Nirgrantha, careless in his walk, might hurt or displace or injure or kill living beings.
>
> A Nirgrantha who is careless in laying down his utensils of begging, might hurt or displace or injure or kill all sorts of living beings. Hence a Nirgrantha is careful in laying down his utensils . . .
>
> If a Nirgrantha would eat and drink without inspecting his food and drink, he might hurt and displace or injure or kill all sorts of living beings. Hence a Nirgrantha eats and drinks after inspecting his food and drink, not without doing so.
>
> This is, Sir, the first great vow: Abstinence from killing any living beings.[2]

Other vows included abstinence from lying, stealing, sexual pleasures, and attachment to sounds, sights, smells, tastes, and feelings of any material objects. All of these vows relate to reverence toward life, but with a humane emphasis. In Jainism, the doctrine of ahimsa was extended to include even the non-sentient world — thus rocks and trees have spirits that must not be injured or maligned.

The origin of ahimsa has had various explanations. Though Radhakrishna and Moore imply that the Jains originated the practice of ahimsa in reaction to Hindu sacrifices,[4] Crooke and Barth hold that Buddhism first developed the concept.[5] I feel there is ample evidence, however, to justify the view of Dasgupta and Jacobi that ahimsa was developed in the obscure past of ancient Hinduism.[6]

The Law of Manu hints at the concept:

> 7. Taking what has not been given, injuring without the sanction of the law.

> 11. That man who keeps this threefold control with respect to all created beings and wholly subdues desire and wrath, thereby assuredly gains complete success.[7]

The early Chandogya Upanishad comments that

> He who is harmless [ahimsant] toward all things elsewhere than at holy places — he, indeed, who lives thus throughout his length of life, reaches the Brahma-world and does not return hither again — yea, he does not return hither again.[8]

The Mahabharata states:

> I know morality, which is eternal, with all its mysteries. It is nothing else than that ancient morality which is known to all, and which consists of universal friendliness, and is fraught with beneficence towards all creatures or upon a minimum of such harm, is the highest morality.[9]

And in the ever-popular Bhagavad-Gita we find:

> Non-violence, truth, freedom from anger, renunciation, tranquility, aversion to fault finding, compassion to living beings, freedom from covetousness.[10]

Ahimsa is an important thread in the fabric of Jain philosophy. The dualistic realism of the Jain is divided into the *jiva* or life principle and the *ajiva* or the world of nature — time, space, law, and the material world. By practicing the ahimsa ethic, a Jain may be able to loosen ties with the material world and finally become liberated from *ajiva*. As previously noted, this also results in greater "light" and freedom from darkness. The intensity of light in man's monad-crystal is in direct proportion to his obedience to ahimsa. Ahimsa not only includes kind treatment to lower forms of life, but the avoidance of lying, stealing, adultery, etc., which would injure other living beings, strengthen ties to the material world, and promote darkness in his mind rather than the light that should be within.[11]

Though monks live a highly refined version of ahimsa, laity do have a vow of ahimsa known as "anubrata" or "small vow," which prohibits meat eating and the killing of annoying insects.

Buddhists have practiced ahimsa since the days of Gautama. The great monastic order, the Sangha, has as its first vow to refrain from destroying life. Asoka, one of India's foremost rulers, was converted to Buddhism and helped spread his faith over much of the East. One rule adopted by Asoka was to eliminate meat from the royal diet. In A.D. 559, Asoka decreed that many animals were to be protected.

In more recent times a well-known advocate of ahimsa was the Indian leader, Mahatma Gandhi. Gandhi had been a lax Hindu until he came under the influence of a Jain priest. After he had made a vow to abstain from sex, wine, and meat, his mother allowed him to go to England to school. At law school in London, Gandhi became a strong supporter of the vegetarian movement.[12]

A Westerner who was strongly influenced by the Eastern concept of ahimsa was Albert Schweitzer. In his work *Civilization and Ethics,* Schweitzer develops his ethical standard of "reverence for life." His motivation did not come from the West but from the Hindu-Buddhist-Jain practice of ahimsa.[13] It is interesting to note that the vegetarian and humane movements exhibit a great deal of consternation in their literature on the lack of support from Christian churches. The reason for this discrepancy between Eastern and Western views is one of our concerns as we survey the Western view of life.

The Hebrews have had a well-established tradition of reverence for life, referred to as Tsa'ar Ba'ale Hayim.[14] The Deuteronomic concern for animals was an integral part of the sacrificial rite. The animal was to be killed in the most efficient and painless manner then known and with a sacrificial attitude. The practical acceptance of man's obvious superiority over animals and the Jewish pragmatic approach to life in general influenced later Christian thought. There is no evidence of a viable vegetarianism in Judaism nor a strong pacifist concern for human life.

The gnostics and some individual Greeks were strong advocates of reverence for life in early Western culture. Though some Greeks viewed man as the Hebrews did, many intellectuals felt that the material body was something to escape from. Others almost worshipped physical beauty. There were four Greeks who are remembered as having a strong influence on man's treatment of animals.

Pythagoras (570-470 B.C.) was a Greek philosopher whose ideas influenced Plato and the fields of mathematics and mysticism. His doctrine of metempsychosis was a basis for treating animals kindly. Pythagoras held that animals had souls of past or future humans, therefore eating animal flesh was unnatural and unlawful since animals were "fraternal" beings.[15]

Plutarch, of biographical fame, also wrote ethical treatises, at least three of which express concern for animals. He advocated vegetarianism from a moral point of view. Plutarch also advised:

> Be as humane as you can . . . Cause as little suffering as possible . . . Kindness and beneficence should be extended to creatures of every species . . . We should be merciful to other creatures. For my own part I would not sell even an old ox.[16]

An early critic of Christianity in the latter part of the second century was Celsus, recorded mainly in Origen's *Contra Celsum*. One of Celsus' favorite points of criticism was the Judeo-Christian idea that man was the center of the universe. With sharp insight and irony, he argued that animals, not man, were the center of the universe. In his view, everything was created not in the interest of something else, but to contribute to the harmony of the whole in order that the world might be absolutely perfect.[17]

The third-century neo-Platonist, Plotinus, taught the concept of an animating force within animals being human in nature or at least a radiation from the all-soul.[18] Either explanation gave ample reason for concern for animal rights.

Porphyry was an ardent disciple of Plotinus. Born in Tyre about A.D. 232, he commented in his treatise "Abstinence from Animal Food":

> Since justice consists in not injuring anything, it must be extended as far as to every animated creature. He who is led by reason does not confine harmless conduct to men alone, but extends it to other animals and is so more similar to divinity.[19]

The New Testament contains very little impetus to advocate reverence for animal life, though it is the epitome of concern for humanity. There are references to the attention paid to the five sparrows being sold for two farthings, "not one of them is forgotten before God." (Luke 12:6) The value judgment is stated, however, that men are worth more than many sparrows. (Matthew 10:31) Vegetarianism is discouraged when Paul reminds Timothy that meat was created by God to be received "with thanksgiving." (1 Timothy 4:1-5) Some, however, did teach vegetarianism as a "council of perfection" (*Teachings of the Apostles* 6:2). Concurrently, the Manicheans remind us of the Jains in that they abstained from eating meat on the grounds that it produced darkness within them while vegetables produced light.[20]

As traditional Christianity developed, we discovered some individual advocates of reverence for life. Bishop Basil of Ceasarea was one of the first Christians who advocated animals having spirits or souls. Basil's telestial creatures were aquatic beings with no spirits; terrestrial animals had spirits but were limited because their heads pointed to the earth. Man, on the other hand, had a head that pointed up, thus indicating his celestial nature. Terrestrial animal spirits would not share in the survival of death with the celestial human.[21] Boethius, around the turn of the sixth century, was very fond of animals but believed they were earthbound.

At the beginning of the thirteenth century, Giovanni Francesco Bernardone became the patron saint of animals as he made Assisi famous. But the theological die was cast when Origen contended with Celsus. Animals were made for man — period. Augustine chided the Manicheans, as Origen did Celsus, for asserting that animals were worthy of any consideration except as providers of food, labor, and clothing for man. Augustine did admit that they brought about one benefit — forcing people to live together in groups. Though man can learn some lessons by watching animals, the beasts themselves lack the divine qualities of reason and free will.[22]

In the thirteenth century Aquinas advocated kindness with a caution. The important thing is not the rights or feelings of the animals, but the attitude of man that needs training.[23] This became the standard rationale for mainline Christianity. What usually only theologians realize is that Francis of Assisi became a saint in spite of his love for animals — not because of it. As a modern Catholic editorial points out, there is a danger in showing much concern for animals. The "empathetic fallacy" of humane societies and a reverence for life of a lower nature than man is actually a sin. When old ladies leave a thousand dollars to care for their pets while there are suffering people, it is a sin. Our attention should be towards God, any efforts less than this may go towards our fellow humans — but never to a lesser form of life. Since animals do not have souls nor will they be resurrected, we should not be attracted to the lower material but to things spiritual.[24] Except for rare individuals such as John Wesley, who believed otherwise, there were very few Christians who stood against the vast majority who had no reverence for animal life. There were some important individuals, such as the philosopher Pierre Bayle, who spoke for animal rights independent of the church of the time and argued that animals had an eternal soul.[25]

Thomas More's plan for a Utopia included the ethical precept that hunting animals should be abandoned. Believing cruelty to animals "had no affinity with true and right feelings," he relegated butchers to the lowest rung in society.[26]

Jeremy Bentham advocated forbidding "every kind of cruelty exercised towards animals." Common in England during his life in the eighteenth century were cockfights, bullbaiting, and hunting hares and foxes — all of which tended to dull the sensibilities of mankind. Bentham contended that "the question is not, can they reason nor, can they talk, but can they suffer?"[27]

William Hogarth presented a graphic study of human cruelty to animals and mankind in his engravings *Four Stages of Cruelty*. The first of the four depicted the pleasure men received from torturing animals. In the remaining scenes, Hogarth portrayed what he felt was the result of cruelty to animals — cruelty to other human beings.[28] Hogarth's engravings have been credited for motivating later English legislation protecting animals.

Vegetarianism has had many early advocates in the Western world, many of whom were concerned about the suffering of animals. Men such as John Evelyn, Thomas Tryon, Alexander Pope, John Wesley, Henry Clubb, W. A. Alcott, Amos Bronson Alcott, and Sylvester Graham were all publishing vegetarians. William Metcalfe was a leader in the vegetarian Bible Christian

Church, which had moved from England to Philadelphia in the early nineteenth century.[29]

Though some individual clergymen, such as Joseph Butler, John Hildrop, Soame Jenyns, Capel Barrow, John Wood, Earnest Bell, E. D. Buckner (who thought he was alone), Agnes Carr and Richard Dean, followed John Wesley in believing that animals had souls and would be resurrected, the majority followed the Reverend Peter Browne, who ridiculed the idea by saying the resurrection of animals was inconceivable and that God would never allow cheese weevils to flourish in heaven.[30]

Concern for animals was first officially expressed in America by articles ninety-two and ninety-three of the Massachusetts Bay Colony's puritan Body of Liberties. The code stipulated that "no man shall exercise any Tirrany or Crueltie towards any bruite Creature which are usually kept for man's use."[31] Thomas Paine and James O'Kelley led the way for such leaders as Henry Bergh, who founded the American Society for the Prevention of Cruelty to Animals 10 April 1866 in New York. George Bancroft was a strong supporter of the movement. George T. Angell organized the Massachusetts SPCA in 1868 and founded the first zoophilic periodical in the world, *Our Dumb Animals*.[32]

The development of these movements was motivated by a variety of factors: (1) There was a concern for "rights" of animals as living creatures as advocated by Porphyry and Thomas Paine and the contemporary James Rachels and Peter Singer. (2) Empathy for the suffering of other beings was emphasized by many following Jeremy Bentham and Eastern ahimsa. (3) Vegetarianism was the motivation of Plutarch and Pope. (4) A utilitarian social benefit appears to be the prime motivation of Hogarth, More, Montaigne, and Aquinas as they saw men practising kindness (or cruelty) on animals and thus becoming trained in their relationships with humans. (5) A feeling of familial relationship is evident among many evolutionists, modern ecologists, Celsus, Pythagoras, and the Hindu tradition. (6) Finally, and probably the least influential in the Western world, is the religious doctrine of animals having souls, being immortal, or being protected by commands not to kill.[33] It is the religious aspect that we will now pursue as we explore some Christian denominations and the Latter-day Saint view in particular.

Vegetarianism among Christian denominations has not always led to a developed sense of reverence for life. The United Society of Believers in the Second Appearing of Christ, commonly called Shakers, were a notable exception. Though "Mother" Ann Lee once taught that dogs had evil spirits and thus were not allowed in homes nor were children to play with them, she later taught "justice and kindness to all the brute creation." Claiming revelations from their deceased Shaker leader, Philemon Steward advocated "holy laws of Zion" which included kindness to animals. Many Shakers did not follow this injunction. H. L. Eads, Bishop of South Union, Kentucky, argued strenuously for the healthiness of eating pork as opposed to the vegetarian faction.[34]

Joseph Smith developed a concern for animals through his efforts at revising the Bible. Whereas William Metcalfe of the Bible Christians altered the punctuation of Genesis 9:5, the Prophet changed it dramatically to read: "And surely, blood shall not be shed, only for meat, to save your lives; and the blood of every beast will I require at your hands." This concept of being judged for our treatment of animals was repeated in the Doctrine and Covenants 49:21 (interestingly intended as a response to Shaker doctrine but given before they practiced vegetarianism). Zion's Camp offered the first practical application of this principle when they were confronted with rattlesnakes on at least two occasions. Joseph Smith and Brigham Young both advised the avoidance of harm to the snakes.[35]

When the Prophet questioned the meaning of animals in heaven as described in Revelation 4, the Lord taught the Prophet a reason for concern. Animals do have spirits, they will be resurrected, enjoy eternal felicity being "full of knowledge," and have power to move about the heavens. (D&C 77:2-4) Preaching a sermon on the subject of animal resurrection, Joseph Smith touched the heart of Jedediah Grant, who had believed John Wesley but had not found a proponent until then.[36]

Reverence for life has always been present in sermons and writings of Latter-day Saint leaders. In fact, they stand out as a peculiar people in the Christian world today. Brigham Young led out strongly in sustaining Joseph Smith's advocacy of reverence for animal life. Reproving hunters for killing more than they could eat, he taught that "these creatures of God" were to be treated with kindness so that "peace [will] increase, and the savage nature of the brute creation [will] vanish away."[37] His counsel to a man with a dying horse "never to destroy life" found echo in the words of President Joseph F. Smith. President Smith, the most prolific advocate of the humane movement among the Church's presidents, instituted a humane day program in the Sunday School for the first Sunday in February.[38] For many years the February issue of the *Juvenile Instructor* carried up to twenty pages of humane material. Its founder and longtime editor and publisher, George Q. Cannon, counselor to three presidents of the Church, has been the strongest advocate for reverence for animal life in the Church's history.[39] President David O. McKay, Joseph Fielding Smith, and Spencer W. Kimball have all made strong pleas for a concern for animal life.[40]

With this background, we shall make some general comments. Eastern ahimsa is a far more integrated way of life in the Eastern culture than the humane movements in the Western world. Some philosophical premises are not as far apart as the religious or ethical codes have become in practice. The recognition of grades of living creatures is found in both cultures. Jains, however, find no authority great enough to warrant killing any living creature. Judeo-Christians and naturalistic humanists, on the other hand, have generally accepted the fact that the lower forms of life may be sacrificed for the higher human needs. With the West believing in the survival of the fittest, whether physically or spiritually, we find the destruction of other human life in order to preserve the righteous achievers or believers. Indeed, killing may be rewarded if commanded by civil or religious leaders. This does not mean a disregard for living things, but rather understanding that short-term suffering or punishment may be beneficial in the long term (1 Nephi 4:13). Suffering and punishment, to the Western mind, is not as absolutely evil as in the Eastern traditions.[41]

One last comment. What is the source of this common denominator — even though seen in various capacities? As Professor

Palmer has so ably pointed out,[42] similarities in religious principles or practices may be explained by (1) man's common spirit; their *''primordial images''* from a premortal existence are manifesting themselves. (2) *The devil invention* theory proposes that the forces of evil are trying to deceive humanity with false counterfeits. This is a popular view among many religions. (3) *Diffusion* or the sharing of ideas by cross-cultural assimilation became popular as the result of nineteenth-century German scholarship. (4) A psychological explanation is that people are similar in their make-up and therefore develop common answers to a *common human predicament*. (5) Another religious explanation is found among the Latter-day Saints with the claim that *the light and spirit of Christ* inspires all men in the same way. (6) Finally, there is the explanation that revelation may come to all nations from God who gives all that His wisdom ''seeth fit that they should have.'' (Alma 29:8) For the Lord commands ''all men to write the words which I speak unto them'' and they will be judged according to their ability to live the words which they have been given. (2 Nephi 29:11) Recognizing that there may be some truth in all explanations, I am strongly partial to the last explanation. I think ahimsa can be regarded as a common denominator in our efforts to relate to some of the children of our Father in heaven who live in Asia.

NOTES

1. *Akaranga Sutra* I:8:1-4, translated by Hermann Jacobi as found in F. Max Muller, ed., *Sacred Books of the East XXII* (Oxford: Clarendon Press, 1884), pp. 79-87.

2. Ibid., II:15:1-5.

3. Ibid., I:4:2:v.

4. Sarvepalli Radhakrishnan, *Indian Philosophy I* (New York: Macmillan, 1929), p. 148 and Radhakrishnan and George E. Moore, ed., *A Source Book in Indian Philosophy* (Princeton, N.J.: Princeton University Press, 1957), p. 251.

5. William Crooke, *Religion and Folklore of Northern India* (London: Oxford University Press, 1926), pp. 103-104 and A. Barth: *The Religions of India,* (London: Kegan Paul, Trench, Trubner, and Company, Ltd., 1921), pp. 97, 139.

6. Surendranath Dasgupta, *A History of Indian Philosophy II* (Cambridge: Cambridge University Press, 1957), pp. 506-511. Jacobi *Op. Cit.,* SBE XXII, pp. xxii-xxxv.

Radhakrishnan and Moore, *A Source Book in Indian Philosophy,* p. 173.

8. Ibid., p. 77.

9. Ibid., pp. 264-65.

10. Ibid., p. 152.

11. Heinrich Zimmer, *Philosophies of India* (New York: Pantheon, 1951), pp. 249-57.

12. Haridas T. Muzumdar, *Mahatma Gandhi* (New York: Charles Scribner's Sons, 1952), p. 10-23 and Mahatma Gandhi: *All Men Are Brothers* (New York: UNESCO, 1958), p. 89.

13. Albert Schweitzer, *Civilization and Ethics* (3rd ed.) (London: Adam & Charles Black, 1949), pp. 240-72.

14. Noah J. Cohen, *Tsa'ar Ba'ale Hayim – The Prevention of Cruelty to Animals: Its Bases, Development and Legislation in Hebrew Literature,* (Washington, D.C.: The Catholic University of America Press, 1959).

15. Ovid, *Metempsychosis* (Cambridge: Harvard University Press, 1916), pp. 369-93, 399. See also Herbert Strainge Long, *A Study of the Doctrine of Metempsychosis in Greece from Pythagoras to Plato* (Princeton: Princeton University Press, 1948).

16. Plutarch, *Moralia V* in *Lives and Writings* (New York: Colonial Co., 1905), 10:3-16.

17. Origen, "Against Celsus," *Ante-Nicene Fathers* (Grand Rapids: Wm. B. Eerdmans, 1953), 4:541.

18. Plotinus, *Enneads* (Boston: Charles T. Ranford, 1916), p. 39.

19. Porphyry, *On Abstinence From Animal Food* (New York: Barnes and Noble, 1965), pp.109-122.

20. Augustine, "On the Morals of the Manichaeans" in *Nicene and Post-Nicene Fathers,* (New York: Christian Literature Co., 1895), 4:77-86, chaps. 14-17.

21. Basil, "The Haemeron" Homily VIII, in *Nicene and Post-Nicene Fathers,* (New York: Christian Literature Co., 1895), 8:95.

22. Augustine, "Concerning the Statues," *Nicene and Post-Nicene Fathers,* 8:1, 9:395.

23. Aquinas, *Summa Theologica,* pp. 383-84, 510, in *Great Books of the Western World,* (Chicago: Encyclopedia Brittanica, 1959).

24. "Empathetic Fallacy," *America* 101 (August 1959):567.

25. Pierre Bayle, *Historical and Critical Dictionary* (Indianapolis: Bobbs and Merrill, 1965), pp. 213-54.

26. Thomas More, *Utopia* (New York: P. F. Collier & Son, 1910), pp. 200-201.

27. Jeremy Bentham, *The Words of Jeremy Bentham* (New York: Russell and Russell, Inc., 1962), 1:562.

28. Philip P. Hallie, *The Paradox of Cruelty* (Middletown, Connecticut: Wesleyan University Press, 1969), pp. 20-33.

29. Gerald E. Jones, "Concern for Animals as Manifest in Five American Churches: Bible Christian, Shaker, Latter-day Saint, Christian Scientist and Seventh-Day Adventist" (unpublished dissertation, Brigham Young University, 1972), pp. 12-17.

30. Ibid., pp. 18-22.

31. Emily Steward Leavitt, *Animals and Their Legal Rights* (New York: Animal Welfare Institute, 1968), p. 13.

32. Francis H. Rowley, *The Humane Idea* (Boston: American Humane Society, 1912), p. 48.

33. Tom Regan and Peter Singer, *Animal Rights and Human Obligations* (Englewood Cliffs: Prentice-Hall, Inc., 1976).

34. H. L. Eads, *Shaker Sermons* (South Union, Ky.: n.n., 1889), p. 334.

35. Joseph Smith, *History of The Church of Jesus Christ of Latter-day Saints*, ed. B. H. Roberts (Salt Lake City: Deseret Book Co., 1959), 2:71.

36. George D. Watt, et. al. (reporters), *Journal of Discourses* (Liverpool: Latter-day Saints Book Depot, 1854), 3, 8, hereafter referred to as *JD*.

37. *JD* 1:203.

38. Gerald E. Jones, ''President Joseph F. Smith and Kindness to Animals,'' *The Animal Stewardship* 1 (August 1973): 6-11.

39. Gerald E. Jones, ''George Q. Cannon: Advocate of Kindness to Animals,'' *The Animal Stewardship* 1 (May, 1973):7-13.

40. Gerald E. Jones, ''The Gospel and Animals'' *The Ensign* 2 (August 1972): 62-65: and ''David O. McKay and Joseph Fielding Smith: Advocates for Animals,'' *The Animal Stewardship* 1 (February 1974): 8-13.

41. John A. Miles, Jr., ''Jain and Judeo-Christian Respect for Life,'' *Journal of the American Academy of Religion* 44 (September 1976): 453-57.

42. Spencer J. Palmer, ''Mormon Views of Religious Resemblances,'' *Brigham Young University Studies* 16 (Summer 1976): 660-81.

6

Why Are There So Many Gods in Japan? Ethos and Pathos in Japanese Religion

Seiji Katanuma

No sooner had I submitted this title than I regretted choosing a difficult topic. I thought of changing my title to: "Why are there so many regrets in my mind?" because it is beyond my ability to make any definite conclusions. Instead, I would like to suggest a scheme which might be helpful within the framework of this panel in stimulating further discussion.

There have been numberless native gods and goddesses in Japan. They are known as kami. They are beasts, natural phenomena, plants and trees, seas and mountains, human beings, and so forth. You might be surprised if you were to hear that there is a strange god, "the ancestor god of electricity — the prince of the excellent magnet," in the Osaka area who is one of the great American inventors, Thomas Edison. These "ridiculous" aspects of ancient Japanese religion are the topic of my discussion. For this purpose, the oldest literature of Japan, the Kojiki, or "Record of Ancient Matters,"[1] should first be carefully studied.

The first character to appear in the Kojiki is the Central Deity of Heaven. This deity does virtually nothing and soon disappears. Immediately after this, the gods of nature come onto the stage.

Generally speaking these gods, who are performing characters on the stage of mythology, are gods with human form. This use of human form is significant and tells us something about the religious mind of the ancient Japanese.

First, the ancient Japanese, according to the Kojiki, abandoned an abstract concept of heaven and metaphysical ideas of the universe. Instead, they preferred to give human form to natural forces. For instance, if a comparison can be made between the mythology of Japan and Greece, a different concept of the so-called "god-nature" relationship would emerge. In Homer's world of Greek mythology, deistic aspects are rarely seen, and they are hidden behind a hedge of human gods. However, the ancient Japanese easily and unrestrainedly bestowed divinity on mountains, seas, and stones, and worshipped them as gods even though they had already accepted the concept of human gods. This duality leads to the question, "What were the gods in Japan?"

After the Central Deity of Heaven disappeared so hurriedly in the Kojiki, the gods of succeeding ages appeared as beings with the highest authority and in the form of the imperial family's ancestors. One of these ancestor gods, Amaterasu Omikami, caused her great light to shine throughout the heavens, as can be seen in the old name of Japan, Toyashihara no Chiaki no Nagaihoaki no Mizuho no Kuni, or "the Fair Land of Reed-Plains and Fifty-Hundred Autumns of Golden Ears of Rice." Amaterasu is also described as a priestess who worships an uncertain supreme existence and who sits down in the sacred weaving room weaving robes of dedication for that uncertain existence now and then.

It is well for me now to introduce some scholarly opinions regarding the essential character of the native gods of Japan in order to provide a premise for grasping a true picture of them. In studying the history of Shinto, the first scholar to offer a feasible definition of the kami was Norinaga Motoori.[2]

He says:

> Kami, or gods, are things like birds, beasts, trees, grasses, the seas and the mountains, whatsoever is fearful and unusual even though they have, on the other hand, beautiful virtues. Kami, in the first place, are gods of heaven, earth, and nature; second, kami are the spirits in the shrines built for

> worshipping them; third, kami are human beings. The phrase "beautiful virtues" means not only "superior virtues" or "honorable virtues," but also wondrous things which are evil or fearful.

This is a good description of the gods in Japan. This explanation of "beautiful virtues" will, I am sure, assist us in understanding the characteristics of the kami.

Mr. Tetsuo Watsuji puts these gods in four main categories:[3] (1) gods who worship the Emperor; (2) gods who worship as well as are worshipped — the ancestor gods of the imperial family; (3) gods who are merely worshipped — the rain god, the wind god, etc.; (4) gods who seek to be worshipped — gods who curse. Dr. Watsuji then concludes: "Gods who worship are superior to those who are worshipped in their divinity."[4]

Tanaka Gen comments on Dr. Watsuji's analysis as follows:

> According to our common sense, that which is worshipped is much superior to that which worships. The most supreme God himself has a positive function from which comes all the world's order and harmony. However, the kami or gods described in the Kojiki or Nihongi (The Chronicle of Japan), are completely different from the type of existence mentioned above. The gods in these works of ancient literature who worshipped others are much superior to those who themselves are worshipped. The qualitative existence which seems to be the highest is a kami whose identity is most ambiguous.[5]

He suggests here that it is necessary to clarify the gods who are identified ambiguously.

Dr. Watsuji explains further:

> Ritual and the administrators of ritual came to hold sanctity as the means for emerging from an infinitely deep mystery. For this reason, they were revered in their divine characters. However, the infinitely deep mystery itself had no opportunity to become translated into gods, even though it made gods what they were by using its might as the hidden unlimited power. . . . That mysterious ultimate is the source of all the gods yet never becomes any particular god. In other words, the source of the gods — the sacred "Nothingness" — is the very thing which does not form any of the gods.[6]

Although Dr. Watsuji's analysis is impressive, it is still vague as to why the Ultimate eventually gave godhood to the Emperor of Japan.

Let us briefly focus on the situation of the first goddess of the imperial family, Amaterasu. Originally the divine "being" representing the godhood of the sun was not Amaterasu alone, but many gods. Some of these gods are: (1) Hoakari no mikoto — the god of fire's light; (2) Amaterukuni teruhiko Hoakari no mikoto — the shining male god of fire's light of the brilliant heaven land; Amaterutakahime no kami, the female supreme god of fire of the brilliant heavens; (4) Hime no kami — female god of fire; (5) Toyohi no kami — the plentiful fire; (6) Asahi toyoakaruhime no kami — female god of plentiful brilliant fires of the morning sun; (7) Amateru maratakeo no kami — the fierce and powerful god of the shining heavens; (8) Amaterumikadono kami — the honorable gateway god of the shining heavens; (9) Amateruya hirume no kami — the female sun god of the resolute shining heavens.

Takeshi Matsumae, a recognized Japanese mythologist, concludes that Amaterasu Omikami of the Ise Grand Shrine, which is the main shrine of the imperial ancestral gods, might be the sun goddess who was originally worshipped by fishermen. His opinion is supported by evidence linking fishermen and boats, as well as boats and the sun in Greek, northern European, Babylonian, Persian and Indian mythology. He observes that "simple, primitive sun gods and goddesses worshipped by fishermen were directed toward the ancestor goddess of the imperial family by the Yamato government in a certain era, probably in the early middle part of the fifth century."[7] My only reservation on this is the fact that Amaterasu Omikami is so closely related to the heavens. She came into existence as a deity when Izanagi no Mikoto (Amaterasu's father, the male god of creation) washed his left eye and told her that she should rule Takamanohara "the plains of Heaven." Amaterasu appeared as the ruler goddess of the plains in heaven.

In the Norito, the ritual chants of the Engishiki, which was compiled from A.D. 905 to 927, there is a useful explanation of how the emperor was so strongly connected with heaven. It says: "The Emperor in every generation, having the holy commands of gods and goddesses, has been delegated to rule over the world."[8] In that context we can easily understand a relationship between Amaterasu and the imperial family. Even though she was merely worshipped by fishermen, as Takeshi Matsumae says, it did not mean that she was the sun goddess having close connections with fishing boats, but that she was the ruler of the world where not only fishermen but also people of every class lived. In other words, in place of the abstract Central Deity in Heaven, the ancient Japanese set and established more concrete, understandable goddesses like Amaterasu as the object of their worship. They acquired a political goddess like Amaterasu by abandoning the somewhat abstract and metaphysical concept attached to the Central Deity of Heaven. Choosing from many available, I would like to introduce an evidential poem written by Kakinomoto no Hitomaro in the early Manyoshu or "Collection of Ten Thousand Poems."[9] It says: "Our Greatest Majesty/ who is the prince of the sun/ which is shining/ all over the heaven/ is going to act/ as if/ he were a god. . . ."[10] That poet certainly understood Amaterasu's background. In Hitomaro's imaginative world of poetry Amaterasu would be a superior deity. Without her, Takama no Hara would be completely dark, as would the Fair Land of Reed-Plains and Fifty-Hundred Autumns of Golden Ears of Rice. Whenever the poets in the days of the Manyoshu sang their verses, not only Kakinomoto but many others used the word *yasumishishi* as a pillow word or modifier, particularly in praising the emperor. Yasumishishi literally means "ruling every corner of the world" or "ruling over the world peacefully."

As I mentioned earlier, Amaterasu has the character of a priestess weaving a sacred robe at the holy weaving room as well as that of a ruler of the world. She therefore belongs to Dr. Watsuji's second classification — a goddess who worships and is worshipped. This characteristic makes her the first ancestor god of the imperial family. If my interpretation is correct, Amaterasu Omikami might be explained conclusively as follows: first, according to descriptions in the Kojiki and Nihongi she is thought to be an existence which should occupy a divine position with holy authority. Therefore, it is incorrect to say that she was merely worshipped by fishermen. Rather, she was the kami of the Yamato tribe who worshipped the sun. The reason why the Yamato tribe developed this religious trend will have to be explained in another paper; the sun goddess might have been a tutelary deity when the Yamato tribe came over the ocean to the islands of Japan from another place.

Second, Amaterasu Omikami, a weaver as well as a ruler, may have been the deity of the Hata or Shin tribe, which was actually the most influential, powerful and skillful group in Japan. In other words, the ancient Japanese put the first ancestor goddess of the imperial family into the position of a priestess, one who could communicate with unknown existence by dedicating offerings and prayers, rather than by delving into the most sacred area of the holy existence and finding out what the Ultimate or Nothingness was.

Third, if my analysis is correct, there might be a new point of view for grasping the reality of Amaterasu Omikami. The word *ama-terasu* has been explained as an honorific form of the expression "ama-teru." As I noted above, there are many gods and goddesses who have the name of "amateru," which literally means "heaven shines or blazes" (intransitive verb). But it is my opinion that the word "ama-terasu" means "to throw light on" or "to illuminate brightly" or "light up" (transitive verb). Such usage can be seen many times in the old literature. For example, note the word *takaterasu* in the Manyoshu.[10] So Amaterasu Omikami was transformed from shining by herself without artificial aids to throwing light throughout the world. She was changed from a mere existence to a conductor. She was changed from the natural to that which affects others. This means that Amaterasu Omikami was indeed transformed into a political ruler of the highest position.

As rice agriculture developed, the religious dignity of the ancestor deities of the imperial family deepened. There was a close parallel between rice production and the prestige of imperial government. In time, Amaterasu Omikami became the epitome of sacred godhood for the Fair Land of Reed-Plains and Fifty-Hundred Autumns of Golden Ears of Rice. And the imperial family in turn became divine over the course of Japanese history because it traced a direct lineage to Amaterasu Omikami.

Shinto was established in this way in a land where the Japanese people had naturally been without doctrines. The core or essential aspect of Shinto, for this reason, came to be explained by only two things, "light" and "darkness."

Japan became a country of great splendor and brightness where the golden rice shafts glittered as they waved in the autumn sun. It was ruled by Amaterasu Omikami and after that by her descendant emperors, all of whom epitomized an environment in which the Japanese people were very happy and active.

The World of Death

The Japanese called the world of death the country of tree-roots. It was the next world to which all would go for a certain time upon leaving this one. The Japanese hated the filth of this world and its shadow of death; they dreamed of a heavenly world after death.

In the Manyoshu few poems speak of death, which is surprising, considering that there are more than 4500 poems in the collection. In examining this oldest collection of poems we find that the ancient Japanese expressed death by such words as *mimikaru* or "to leave one's body," and *kamuagaru* or "to be exalted as a god." This is also the concept of death in the Kojiki. The world of death was regarded as Tokoyo no Kuni or "the everlasting country" which lay far beyond the sea of flowing rice shafts. They pictured a peaceful land where one would be embraced as a mother embraces a child. However, there was no specification as to who would go to the country of roots and who would go to heaven. But for the ancient Japanese people, the concept of death was never of a pessimistic nature.

The Consciousness of Sin

The ancient Japanese were not conscious of sin and evil. Rather, they were conscious of light as opposed to dark, and filthiness as opposed to purity. Killing was a sin, not because it took away the victim's freedom by taking his life, but because it was an unclean act that stained the shining land with blood.

Shinto is not a logical or philosophical system, although Shinto means "the Way of the Gods." As Norinaga Motoori says, there was little discussion of what the Way was. In fact there was little attention paid to it at all. The Japanese followed the Way without consciously recognizing its existence. However, in most foreign countries it has been the custom to debate about many different doctrines and philosophies, some arguing for this way and others arguing for that way. Anciently in Japan there was peace and order because there were no such theories and doctrines in the imperial great eight island country, where the descendants of the sun goddess have consecutively succeeded to the throne.[11]

Living the course of nature, simply and purely, was, I daresay, all that Shinto had to offer by way of religion.

The Influence of Buddhism

Now I would like to discuss Buddhism in Japan. Let me describe an event that occurred in the early days of Buddhism. In the beginning of the sixth century Buddhism came from India to Japan by way of China and the Korean peninsula. This new religion began to steal the hearts of many people. Before fifty years had passed, members of powerful royal and aristocratic families had adopted this religion. In the year A.D. 584, a noble man, Soga no Umako, who might have been a minister of finance, built a small Buddhist sanctuary on his own estate. The following year he built a pagoda on the hill Ono.

The conflict between modern Buddhism and traditional Shinto can be illustrated in the following example: The progressive Soga Clan was in serious conflict with the traditionalist Mononobe Clan, which was once the most powerful clan and protected the god Ninigi, the first god to come down from heaven to Japan. In the year 586 Mononobe Moriya suddenly sent an army to Soga's mansion and burned Soga's pagoda, his small sanctuary, and a statue of Buddha. You can imagine how unpleasant this new Buddhism was to the Mononobe Clan, who believed in the traditional Shinto faith.

However, the powerful crown prince, Shotoku was deeply attracted to Buddhism, and after three volumes of commentaries on Buddhist scripture were produced, Buddhism began to prosper. Are there any religions in the world which were permitted to exist after officially losing a conflict with another religion or after having fought a war against another religion? This is not limited to a few specific religions but extends to those beliefs which would represent a nation. When we study Christianity, Judaism or Islam, for example, we find long histories of violent conflicts.

We are faced with an interesting problem. What became of Shinto after Buddhism spread into Japan on a national scale? How did Buddhism gain its prosperity? In short, how was the Japanese history of religion affected? These questions must be considered very carefully in order to understand the religious consciousness of the Japanese.

It was Mahayana Buddhism that was brought to Japan. I am not a Buddhist specialist, but if my own interpretation may be permitted, it produced a shock within the spiritual life of the ancient Japanese people. I do not have time to discuss this in detail, so I will cover only the main points.

Let me introduce briefly the influence of Buddhism on the ancient Japanese people by citing a poem sung by Yuge no Miko, Prince Yuge.

> As the cloud which hangs over
> The Mifune Mountain
> Must surely pass away,
> I realize that my life
> will not go on forever.[12]

I believe you can feel a tone of ephemerality in the grievous emotion of Prince Yuge's heart.

Another poem is sung by Otomo no Tabito, whose family was once as prestigious as Mononobe, but now fallen.

> In the next world
> It would not matter
> If I became a bird or an insect
> If I could just be happy now.[13]

This poem introduces Buddhist ideas of transmigration and retribution. The poet, who never became the minister of the central government but spent his life as a local officer, was sighing a deep sigh by indulging himself in pleasure and rejecting nirvana. These two poems show a strong Buddhist influence among the Japanese people of ancient times.

Let me illustrate three main ways Mahayana influenced Japanese life. First, Mahayana Buddhism introduced the foreign ideas of individual existence to the Shinto mind of ancient Japan. In the Japanese's inner world, the teaching that "truth is beyond speech and thought, and therefore it is nothingness (sunyata), that all worldy phenomena are illusory" gradually took concrete form. Second, Mahayana Buddhism presented new concepts in understanding the mind. Third, Mahayana Buddhism presented a new view of nirvana or the next world. However, to Shinto, Mahayana Buddhism, with its superior teachings, did not become Shinto's enemy, but rather a teaching "above" and "superior" which could be embraced as a mother embraces her child. Shinto never vanished from Japan, yet at the same time Buddhism influenced the spiritual life of the people. The two continued in a coexisting relationship. This compromise had been carried out skillfully through the so-called theory of "Honji Suijaku," which is said to mean that Buddha (who is called Honji) was brought to Japan by the Shinto gods as Suijaku. But in spite of the religious prosperity of Buddhism, Shinto, the ancestral religion of the imperial family, was still honored. The indigenous Shinto gods held a sacred place for the emperors of every generation. They were the source of political and religious authority.

Briefly speaking, the religious structure of Japan is unique, with its ancestor-god worship which went from family to clan, and clan to emperor, and fit into the political structure, which ran from the emperor to the clan, and from the clan to the family. This structure had a long history which continued until August 15, 1945, the end of World War II. Japan had been defeated by the United States, and on New Year's Day, 1946, the emperor made his so-called "human declaration," in which he declared himself to be human and not a god.

Why had the emperor been worshipped by the Japanese? I would like to relate an account of a round-table discussion, as printed in the June 1937 edition of Shufu no Tomo, or "The

Housewife's Friend.'' The participants, older mothers from farming areas of Japan, had lost sons in the war between Japan and China. One of these mothers said:

> When the call came for our older son to join the war effort, we said again and again, ''We offer our son's life to the great emperor . . . and may it be taken quickly!'' Recently our hopes were realized and the emperor allowed our son to receive an honorable death in the war.

Another woman said:

> The night our son's body was brought into the Yasukini Shrine on a white palaquin, we were so full of thanks we could hardly contain ourselves. Just the thought that this unworthy child should be allowed to receive such an honor . . . it is wonderful!

And another:

> We must thank the Great Emperor for our son's honorable death. It is an honor greater than we deserve!

And still another:

> Now that our son has been taken, we are able to go up to the Yasukini shrine to worship our Great Emperor and receive his praise. We have no regrets. Even if we were to die this very day we would be content. Why, we would die laughing.

And finally:

> Truly when we think that our son will return no more we cannot help feeling lonely but, when we think that he died for our country and that we will receive the admiration of the Emperor, we become so encouraged that we forget all else.

These remarks lead us to an important corollary. I think you could recognize certain characteristics in the remarks of these mothers. Did you recognize the fact that they always said ''we'' or ''our'' in place of using ''I'' or ''my''? Each one had her mura, or ''the place where people gather together,'' where farmers worked the rice fields in the twilight. Humble straw cottages stood along the narrow footpath between rice fields. They had to live in this agricultural area. And rice agriculture demanded the cooperation between family members and people of the village. Even though something bothered someone, he could not leave that mura, because that meant not only leaving his home but abandoning his means of living. Over many generations unconsciousness of "self" had formed. The farmers thought first of their family. The self concept existed somewhere beyond their mura and nation. They had no consciousness of an almighty God who attached importance to a relationship between Himself and individual humans. They were conscious only of an emperor who was head god of a nation containing many muras, and muras containing many families.

Summary

By way of conclusion, I would like to reiterate four basic points. First, the Japanese concept of god is quite different from that of the Christian. In Japanese the word *kami* or *god* merely means above or superior. Second, this had led the Japanese people to a religious generosity in which everything that appears "above" or "superior" easily becomes deified. Third, their attitude toward nature allowed them to produce many gods. Japan, a country of rice production, has been blessed by a beautiful natural environment; but at the same time her people have suffered from the dreadful appearance of typhoons, floods and landslides. This awesomeness of nature, its "beauty" and "havoc," have spontaneously become the people's gods. Fourth, to the ancient Japanese who had lived within an agrarian rice culture, nature was the most evident fact of existence; there was no way to exert power in opposition to it. They learned to harmonize with nature. They also learned that diligence, a characteristic of their stone-like endurance, their agricultural life, helped them enjoy nature. Through such homeopathic sentiment and emotion, they could finally succeed in becoming identified with nature. And in so doing, their Shinto religion, developed along animistic, shamanistic, and polytheistic lines.

NOTES

1. The oldest historical record of Japan, compiled by Ono Yasumaro in A.D. 712. It contains three volumes.

2. A scholar of the Japanese classics. Norinaga's years are 1730-1801.

3. Tetsuo Watsuji, *Nihon Korai Bunka,* Tokyo, Iwanami Shoten, pp. 61-63.

4. Ibid., pp. 64-66.

5. Gen Tanaka, *Kodai Nihonjin no Sekai,* Tokyo, Yoshikawa Kobunkan, p. 19.

6. Tetsuo Watsuji, *Nihon Korai Bunka,* Tokyo, Iwanami Shoten, p. 76.

7. Takeshi Matsumae, *Kamigami no Keifu,* PHP Kenkyusho, p. 62.

8. *Hoshizume no Matsuri* in the *Engishiki.*

9. The oldest collection of Japanese poems. It contains twenty volumes and more than 4500 poems covering approximately four hundred years from A.D. 350 to 759.

10. *Manyoshu,* Vol. 1, No. 45.

11. Norinaga Motoori, *Naobi no Mitama.* Published in 1771.

12. *Manyoshu,* Vol. 3, No. 242.

13. Ibid., Vol. 3, No. 348.

Objectifying Divine Power: Some Chinese Modes

7

Laurence G. Thompson

The general topic of "deity and the divine" is indeed an enormous one, whose thorough exploration would ultimately involve every aspect of the phenomena of religions. If I hope to say anything meaningful about Chinese religion in this regard, it will be necessary to concentrate upon a few selected points. I shall first suggest a standpoint so that you will be able to see where I am coming from, and then I shall try to explicate three major characteristics I find in the Chinese mode of objectifying Divine Power.

A Definition of Religion

There has never been, and doubtless never will be, a general agreement as to what "religion" is; only an agreement perhaps of what *our* religion is. The most liberal definitions of recent decades have even eliminated the minimal requirement of the supernatural in favor of various versions of a concept of ultimacy. Personally, in the study of religions, I am quite agreeable to utilizing the broadest possible definitions as most conducive to breaking through conceptual barriers.

In this paper, I shall adopt the common view that religion can be considered under the aspect either of a universal or of many particulars. There seems to be a universally attested reality in human experience that may be called the irreducible element of religion. That reality has been carefully analyzed by many scholars and summed up in such terms as the "holy," "other-power," or the "sacred."[1] Human experience of this reality has been characterized and explained in various ways: as fear, awe, a thrill, ineffable bliss; as psychologically subjective, or as empirically objective, but in any case, this seems to be the universal level of religious experience.

On the other hand, the *expression* of religion has taken innumerable forms and may be found prominently in societies as well as among individuals. In fact, almost every academic discipline that is concerned with man may be focused, with enlightening results, upon the problems of religion

In all this I am simply expressing, in a somewhat special way, the implications of what Van der Leeuw called "religion as essence and manifestation." Furthermore, if the essence of religion is a universal experience, then the varying manifestations of religion may be understood as the expressions of particular cultures as well as of particular individuals. To clarify this, I am looking at religion as a universal human experience particularized in countless ways in various cultures.[2] To think of religion as some neat package of dogmas, much less as a private possession of any group, is automatically to foreclose on the possibility of understanding either the religions of others, or man as *homo religiosus*.

Western attempts to understand Chinese religion have all too often suffered from precisely this sort of self-defeating provincialism. Even with the best of intentions, the imposition of traditional Western theological categories, for example, has resulted in producing more puzzles than understandings. We need to accept that there are many ways of being religious, and that a phenomenological approach will be essential.

As to our specific subject, I take it that the term "the Divine" is another appellation for the universal experience we have mentioned, whereas the term "Deity" is on the level of the particular. If we are studying Chinese religion, we shall want especially to examine this level of particulars, because that is where the *Chineseness* of religion lies. By the title of my essay I intend to indicate that what I want to do is to elucidate (only very sketchily) a few particular ways in which the universal experience of the Holy, the other-Power, the Sacred, or the Divine come to tangible expression in the Chinese way through notions of Deity.

Three World Views: Chinese, Western, Indian

First I believe it is essential to clarify the fundamental world view of the Chinese tradition. For the sake of simplicity (although not, I trust, simple-mindedness), we might contrast three cosmologies in the three major civilizations of the West, India, and China. In the West, the dominant view could be pictured as a circle representing the universe with God outside and "above." For India, I suppose that the dominant view could be pictured as a circle representing the universe and conterminously God. For China, there would likewise be the circle representing the universe — but without God. The Western view is of a Creator and His creation, two different and distinct entities. The Indian view is of God and His creation as one and the same. The Chinese view is of a universe that functions in accordance with an invariable Way (*Tao*) but without a creator.[3]

In each of these cosmologies there are many implications. Most importantly, they imply relationships between man and the universe, man and Creator. The Western view not only emphasizes the separateness of man and God, but even more importantly, the special position of man in God's creation. Not only is the world created by God especially for man's benefit, but man himself is said to be formed "in the image of God." He is outfitted with a soul that links him directly with his Creator, and the latter maintains a continuing concern for every human soul. In return, every soul should worship its Creator. This gives to the individual in the West significance that is reflected in all of Western history and institutions. Western man has likewise consistently acted out the role claimed for him as master of all the rest of creation. All the world is indeed a stage for his dramatic history. In Western art these suppositions are clearly shown. Man is the great subject, especially man's special relationship to God. Nature is merely the backdrop — unless it is actually man's enemy. Man's worship of his Creator is somehow, because of the cosmology, perilously close to worship of himself.

This brings us exactly to the Indian view. Inasmuch as Creator and creation are one and the same, there can be no separation in fact of man from God, or of man from nature. The world may be a stage, but on it is performed a play of illusions in which God simply enjoys himself. Man's religious task, the only task that can be taken seriously in this cosmology, is to arrive at the realization that he and God are one. The universe is the ocean and individual men are the drops of spray that are tossed up for an instant and then fall back to be reabsorbed in the sea. In such a view there is no room for an exaggerated individualism. Indian religion advises one to "be still, and know you *are* God."

In the Chinese view, man and nature are parts of a great gestalt. There being no Creator, man cannot be a special creation. But equally there being no God, man himself is not God. Whatever the original mythologies of creation (and in China these have been preserved only fragmentarily), the world of the ancient Chinese as far back as we know it seems to be a *given,* functioning spontaneously, coherently, in its own natural way. Because of his reflective capacities, man had a special part to play in this world. He could partially create and partially control, as was attested by his civilization. (This capacity was a source of pride to the Confucian mind and the opposite to the Taoists.) But in the last analysis, man's task was to go harmoniously with the way of the universe; and even the Confucian proponents of civilization concede that this civilization conformed to nature rather than being man's protest against, or conquest of nature. In Chinese art, as in Western, we find the world view clearly reflected. Nature is the great subject; its Way, or *Tao,* is what man sought to immerse himself in.

And so the first of the three characteristics I want to ascribe to Chinese religion arises from the world view. Whereas in India and the West Creative Power was objectified and worshiped, Chinese religion did *not* objectify and worship Ultimate Reality or *Tao*. It remained an abstract concept which evoked a religious attitude only, perhaps, in the recondite liturgy of the Taoist "mass" (*chiao*).[4] We may speak of Taoist mysticism as similar to mystical practice throughout the world, but the attempt "to become one with *Tao*" seems to be less a goal of "union with God" than a hope of attaining personal power — even immortality.

Euhemerization and Diffusion of Divine Power

But if the Ultimate Reality of the universe was not Deity, the Chinese, any more than any other people, could not rest content with philosophical abstractions. In coping with the world, man requires at least the illusion that he can summon help, and hope requires the accessibility of help. A Lao Tzu or a Chuang Tzu might meet the vicissitudes of life with perfect equanimity, like leaves drifting resistlessly on the shifting currents; but for other men, life is a never-ending struggle. Fear of defeat, of loss, of disease, of death, requires hope, which can only come from power stronger than that of mortals. In the world view of the Chinese, there was a level of reality above the mundane where such power existed and could be tapped. It is at this level that deity becomes objectified in ways that are no different than those found in other cultures. That is to say, divine power becomes anthropomorphized.

Euhemerization has often been considered a basic characteristic of Chinese myths and concepts of gods, but I suppose it is not so much a Chinese, as a general human way of conceiving deity. When supernatural power becomes specified, it can hardly be in any other way. Even the most fantastic imaginings of science-fiction writers about beings immeasurably advanced beyond the human species in the end produce only Superman. Religious art must resort to anthropomorphic symbols (even though in rare instance such symbols may avoid direct depiction of the humanized god). The human mind surely finds the manifestations of power that emerge from the supermundane level to be homologous with the power of human wills.

The second major characteristic of Chinese religion I want to discuss is the *diffusion* of divine power. In understanding non-Western religions, Westerners always have difficulty coming to terms with world views that take deity to be multiple rather than single. The stern Old Testament injunctions against polytheism have incalculably damaged Western man's understanding of the rest of mankind — which for the most part has taken for granted that deity was multiple. Secure in his Biblically sanctioned notion that there is only one God and that nothing is more abhorrent than the worship of many gods, Western man has taken fire and sword, as well as his scriptures, to the heathen, primarily to punish this blasphemy.

However, to those who do not come from this tradition of a single jealous God, the diffusion of divine power is logical and obvious. The manifestations of power are infinite and various; nothing would seem more natural than to attribute their causes to many diversified deities. In this world, which is necessarily the model for the supramundane dimension, one approaches different persons for different sorts of results. According to such a view, the power that causes the river to flow is a different power than the one that governs disease, just as the function of the farmer differs from that of the metalsmith.

This being so, we can comprehend why deity in China is anthropomorphized and why it is multiple. We can go beyond the sort of superficial depiction of ''idolatry'' that assumes not only gross ignorance, but a sort of baseness of character in Chinese worship. Objectification of divine power in statues of mud or bronze or wood representing many differently named deities is not a naive belief in the divinity of inanimate objects, but a visual representation of the accessibility of superhuman aid — the aid requested being within the province of power of a particular deity.[5]

The most intriguing question here is: what is the origin of these many and varied deities? We may be excused from attempting to supply an answer, as this subject constitutes one of the major branches of the discipline of history of religions.[6] We feel justified in limiting this discussion to a few salient points that bear upon this topic.

There is first the fact that no one pantheon existed for the whole range of Chinese religion. Here, a Western-style ''systematic theology'' would compile several lists, such as deities in the State cult, deities of Chinese Buddhism, Taoist deities, and deities belonging to the folk cults. Such a classificatory approach has, in fact, often been used in studying Chinese religion, and of course there is no reason to deny its validity. It will not in itself, however, take us very far along the road to a real understanding of the subject.

More interesting is the fact that the power of the deities varies greatly, is for the most part not too potent, and is only slightly removed from that of man himself. In the State cult, the variances of power were clearly set forth by a ranking system that governed the sacrifices. In fact, the ruler of men was likewise the ruler of gods. He acknowledged only the ultimate Power of Heaven and Earth — and his ancestors — as higher than his own. All other numina, like his mortal subjects, owed their ranks and titles to the emperor's decree and were promoted or demoted like his human officials.[7] This indicates that for the most part, the concept of "deity" is closely related to, if not in fact a form of, the concept of human spirits or ghosts.

Such an interpretation is supported by the findings of a number of anthropologists who have recently been at work on "gods, ghosts, and ancestors" in the current folk religion in Taiwan and Hong Kong. Their most general conclusion would seem to be that, in essence, these are but variations of the same theme, namely, that supernatural power is exercised by deceased human beings. That ghosts and ancestors are deceased humans is obvious by definition; but that folk gods are likewise originally human is a striking demonstration of the ancient theory of Euhemerus. The most challenging version of these findings is the hypothesis of Philip Baity, which surmises that the community gods were originally ghosts, propitiated by the community out of fear, and eventually becoming objects of hope rather than fear.[8] The folk religion, in any case, thus takes divine power as quite akin to, and only slightly more potent than, that of the mortal powers of this world.

Thus we see that the gods are familiar beings, existent in the invisible dimension, but not of some unthinkably different character than men. They are not so high and mighty as to be unapproachable by ordinary mortals, and they are accessible through sacrifice and prayer by the common folk. Perhaps this is why so much of the folk religion operates without the services of an ordained priesthood.

This relative intimacy and near-equality of gods and men was brought about, or at least maintained, by the age-old assumption that spiritual beings need the support of mortals and vice versa. Not only do spirits need the nourishment of sacrifices, but they depend for their very existence upon the continuing faith of men. In fact, they would have had no existence at all but for this faith, and the Chinese are tough-minded enough to believe that unless a deity responds positively to prayer, he is either powerless or should be left to pass unremembered into oblivion. Divine power must manifest itself, or for all practical purposes it does not exist.

The Nature of Evil

The two major characteristics of Chinese religion discussed thus far seem fairly unambiguous to me, but there is a third characteristic that may be more problematical. That is the nature of evil.

Many religions have, of course, emphasized the duality of divine power and have even personified the struggle between good and evil as the ultimate dynamic of the world. The transcendental struggle then becomes objectified in the world of men, who must make a religious choice between God and the devil.

There is no difficulty in finding evil in the human world of the Chinese and no difficulty either in finding evil in the supramundane dimension. A high proportion of the evil that befalls men is attributable to the impingement of the latter upon the former. A prominent aspect of Chinese religion is what de Groot called "the war against spectres," and his "demonology" is as exhaustive as one can find for any culture.[9] Among the many varieties are water-demons, ground-demons, animal-demons of numerous species, plant-demons, and spectres of mountain and forest. These spectres, commonly called *kuei,* are omnipresent and always dangerous, and man must continually guard against their depredations by both magical and religious techniques.

Can we find in Chinese religion a transcendental struggle between good and evil objectified in the world of man? On the one hand it seems that we can, as we consider that there are two eternally interacting forces which produce this ever-changing phenomenal world — the famous *yin* and *yang*. In the folk religion of China, *yang* stands for good and *yin* for evil. On the other hand, *yin* and *yang* are not entities or beings or deities. They are never personified in and of themselves but are concepts adduced in describing conditions and changes in the material world. One might say that *yin-yang* is a dialectic of power, but not of *divine* power.

Still, evil is characterized as *yin* and is objectified in the form of specific spirits in the folk religion. People are sometimes taken over by such evil spirits, which must be exorcised by specialists using *yang* instruments.[10] Does this mean that there is in Chinese religion the concept of a principle of evil at large in the cosmos of which malevolent spirits are agents?

So far as I can judge at present, it does not. There seems to be no theory about transcendental evil in the ancient literature, nor (although the canon has as yet remained too little studied to say for sure) does it appear to be found in the Taoist texts. As for Buddhism, although it came into China with a rich repertory of novel ideas including karmic destiny, punishments in purgatory, and various levels of existence, it seems to me not to have a principle of evil as such. The devil in Buddhism is *Māra,* who symbolizes the inevitability of death — and thence rebirth into suffering — for those who remain attached to the samsaric world; in other words, Māra stands for ignorance or illusion. The Karmic cycle with death as both end and beginning is, of course, evil, but *Māra's* polar opposite is not good, but unattachment or enlightenment. *Māra,* in other words, is no more an entity or deity than *yin* or *yang* but is a concept descriptive of the condition of man still doomed to rebirth through failure to let go of ego. It is an evil *state,* not an evil being. (Such is my understanding of *Māra,* but it is subject to correction by specialists. It may be correct as it stands at a certain level of Buddhist teaching but may not give enough consideration to the folk level.)

Then what is the source of the countless malign spirits of Chinese religion? I am inclined to think that all evil spirits are, in the last analysis, the ghosts of humans. They derive from the root of Chinese religion, which is the ancestral cult. In that cult, it is essential that the deceased be remembered by the sacrifices of their descendants. When for any reason an ancestral spirit is deprived of its due sacrifices — is what I have called a bereaved spirit — it becomes hungry and homeless and feels the anguish of abandonment. It may try to get the sacrifices to which it is entitled by plaguing its living descendants with bad luck of all kinds. It may become a public nuisance, even a menace to the community.

The strength of the belief in this danger from bereaved spirits is seen in the fact that the entire seventh month is considered a time when they must be appeased and hopefully propitiated. (They are joined, indeed, by the Buddhist ghosts of the damned who are on parole from purgatory during that month. The two species of ghosts seem to be assimilated into a general category.) The situation of the bereaved spirits is vividly expressed in the prayer offered on behalf of the emperor during official sacrifices in Ming and Ch'ing times:

> . . . These lonely souls have no one on whom to depend in death. Their *yang*-souls (*ching-shen*) have not yet dispersed [to Heaven], but remain attached to their *yin*-souls (*yin-ling*), and so they live in plants or trees, act as uncanny bogies, howl dismally beneath the stars and moon, and moan in the wind and rain. Whenever there is a religious festival among men, they think about this *yang* world, and the souls — lost in darkness, never to return, their bodies perished — long anxiously for sacrifices.[11]

Such bereaved spirits were malevolent for the most understandable of reasons. But they were not evil manifestations of a divine power of evil, or even originally by nature evil. They were victims of neglect, of a situation in which the proper relationship between the living and dead had been disrupted. They could be pacified and turned from devils into gods by the simple act of restoring their sustaining offerings.[12] As the classical text taught, "When a ghost [*kuei*] has a place to go [another word also pronounced *kuei*], it does not become an evil spirit."[13]

Whether further study will prove or disprove the theory that the only source of evil spirits in Chinese religion is neglect of ancestral sacrifices, I think it safe to say that the third major characteristic in our analysis can be identified as the lack of a conflict of good and evil at the transcendental level and the consequent lack of objectification of evil at the level of deity.

Summary

In what has been presented so briefly here, we do not, of course, intend to suggest a complete theory of Chinese religion, which is a subject of vast proportions as yet only spottily investigated. But presuming that the objectification of divine power is one of the most fundamental aspects of religion, we may hope to have opened up the subject for more adequate treatment. In summary, we have suggested that three modes of objectification are especially conspicuous: first, that Ultimate Reality (that is, *Tao*) is *not* objectified; second, that divine power is exercised through many kinds of deities who are for the most part human in origin and as dependent upon man as man is upon them; third, that divine power in China knows no transcendent struggle between good and evil. None of this represents any original discovery by the author, but our purpose will be achieved if this essay stimulates further and more profound studies along these lines.

NOTES

1. See such famous works as Rudolf Otto, *The Idea of the Holy;* G. van der Leeuw, *Religion as Essence and Manifestation;* Mircea Eliade, *The Sacred and the Profane, Patterns in Comparative Religion.*

2. Again, this particular sort of definition is used here because of the requirements of the topic as set and not necessarily because I think it is the most adequate.

3. For the Chinese view, see especially Joseph Needham, *Science and Civilization in China,* Vol. II (Eng.: Cambridge University, 1956), chapter 18, "Human Law and the Laws of Nature in China and the West." See also his "Human Law and the Laws of Nature," in the collection of his essays entitled *The Grand Titration* (Toronto: University of Toronto Press, 1969).

4. Only within the last few years have we become acquainted with this most sophisticated and profound of all rituals at the folk level. See, in English, especially the book of Michael Saso, *Taoism and the Rite of Cosmic Renewal* (Washington State University, 1972), chapter 4 in particular.

5. For a particularly helpful discussion of the problem discussed in the foregoing three paragraphs, see Wax, Murray & Rosalie, "Magic and Monotheism," in June Helm, editor, *Symposium on New Approaches to the Study of Religion,* Proceedings of the 1964 Annual Spring Meeting of the American Ethnological Society, University of Washington (1964), pp. 50-60.

6. For a comprehensive summary and bibliography, see Charles H. Long, "Primitive Religions," in Charles J. Adams, ed., *A Reader's Guide to the Great Religions* (New York, 2nd edition 1977), pp. 1-38.

7. The most thorough explication of this subject is by C. K. Yang. See his book, *Religion in Chinese Society* (University of California, 1961), chapter 8.

8. See Baity's book, *Religion in a Chinese Town* (Taipei, 1975) chapter 6. Also see his article, "The Genesis of Gods in Taiwanese Folk Religion: A Preliminary Analysis," in Harry Partin, comp., *Asian Religion-History of Religion: 1974,* pre-printed papers from the 1974 meeting of the American Academy of Religion.

9. J. J. M. de Groot, *The Religious System of China* (Leiden, 1892-1910; reprinted in Taipei, 1964). See especially volumes 5 and 6.

10. See Peter Goullart's book, *The Monastery of Jade Mountain* (London, 1961) chapter 9; or Laurence G. Thompson, *Chinese Reli-*

gion: An Introduction, 2nd ed. (Encino & Belmont, California, 1975), pp. 29-32, including material extracted from Goullart's account.

11. Quoted in Laurence G. Thompson, "Yu Ying Kung: the Cult of Bereaved Spirits in Taiwan," in Laurence G. Thompson, ed., *Studia Asiatica* (San Francisco, 1975), p. 271.

12. The matter is not so straightforward as these words suggest. There is an intriguing problem currently being discussed by scholars concerning the functioning of *feng-shui,* or the geomantic siting of dwellings for the living and dead, that would have to be considered in a full treatment. The point is that if *feng-shui* operates "automatically," then the willful or religious element in the operations of the dead upon their descendants is minimized or eliminated — which would change our conclusion accordingly. This view that *feng-shui* works "scientifically" rather than "religiously" is held by Maurice Freedman, Jack Potter, and other anthropologists. We refrain from citing the literature, which would take us too far afield.

13. *Tso Chuan,* Duke Chao's 7th year (B.C. 534). For the whole setting of the quotation, see James Legge, *The Chinese Classics,* 5: 618.

Symposium Participants

W. Ananda, International Buddhist Center (Colombo, Sri Lanka), "Buddhist Ceremonies in Sri Lanka"

R. Lanier Britsch, Brigham Young University (Provo, Utah), Panel Chairman, "Ways of Worship"

C. Paul Dredge, Northeastern University (Boston, Massachusetts), "What's in a Funeral? Korean, American-Mormon, and Jewish Rites Compared"

Sami A. Hanna, University of Utah (Salt Lake City, Utah), "Death and Dying in the Middle East"

Jeffrey R. Holland, Church Commissioner of Education, The Church of Jesus Christ of Latter-day Saints (Salt Lake City, Utah), luncheon address, "Of Countries and of Kingdoms"

Paul V. Hyer, Brigham Young University, Discussant

Sechin Jagchid, Brigham Young University, Discussant

Edward T. Jones, University of Minnesota (Minneapolis, Minnesota), "A Comparative Examination of Ascension Motifs in World Religions"

Gerald E. Jones, Institute of Religion, The Church of Jesus Christ of Latter-day Saints (Berkeley, California), "Reverence for Life in Religion: Eastern and Western Views"

Seiji Katanuma, Hokkaido National Educational University, Iwamawa Campus (Hokkaido, Japan), "Why Are There So Many Gods in Japan?"

Truman G. Madsen, Brigham Young University, "Distinctions in the Mormon Approach to Death and Dying"

Merlin G. Myers, Brigham Young University, Panel Chairman, "Death and Dying"

Hugh Nibley, Brigham Young University, Discussant

Spencer J. Palmer, Brigham Young University, Symposium Chairman, "Confucius on a Tatami: Japanese Adaptations of a Chinese Cult"

Laurence G. Thompson, University of Southern California (Los Angeles, California), "Objectifying Divine Power: Some Chinese Modes"

Douglas F. Tobler, Brigham Young University, Panel Chairman, "Deity and the Divine"

C. Terry Warner, Brigham Young University, Discussant

Masakazu Watabe, University of Southern California, Discussant

Gary S. Williams, Brigham Young University, "Taoist Rituals in Taiwan"

Local Arrangements:

Estelle Farmer
Robert Norton
John Stephenson
Wendell Wheeler
Elizabeth Wilkinson

Index